S0-BYP-848

Book may be kept

FOURTEEN DAYS

charged for each day

WITHDRAWN
L. R. COLLEGE LIBRARY

CHRISTIAN
EDUCATION
OF
ADULTS

# CHRISTIAN EDUCATION
## OF
# ADULTS

*by*

EARL F. ZEIGLER

*Published for the*
COOPERATIVE PUBLISHING ASSOCIATION
*by*
THE WESTMINSTER PRESS
*Philadelphia*

Carl A. Rudisill Library
LENOIR RHYNE COLLEGE

268.434
Z e 3 c

© W. L. JENKINS MCMLVIII

*All rights reserved* — no part of this book may be reproduced in any form without permission in writing from the publisher, except by a reviewer who wishes to quote brief passages in connection with a review in magazine or newspaper.

This is one of a series of books produced for interdenominational use by the Protestant denominations working through the Cooperative Publishing Association.

Scripture quotations from the Revised Standard Version of the Bible are copyright, 1946 and 1952, by the Division of Christian Education of the National Council of Churches, and are used by permission.

Library of Congress Catalog Card No. 58–5517

36648
August 1958

PRINTED IN THE UNITED STATES OF AMERICA

# CONTENTS

# FOREWORD

This book has been written at the invitation of the Co-operative Publishing Association to provide a text for Course 412b — *Christian Education of Adults*. Its style, however, has been purposefully selected to interest the leaders of adults in the local churches who may or may not enroll in a study course. The book covers the general field of adult Christian education, and the author has tried not to encroach too much on other books in the series. He is indebted to denominational directors of adult work and adult editors for valuable information about their respective activities and programs, and he takes this opportunity of thanking them for their willing co-operation. Gratitude is also due Dr. Edward K. Trefz, associate director of adult program in the Presbyterian U.S.A. Board of Christian Education, who wrote Chapter VII on the young adults. His responsibilities in this field made him particularly welcome to the author as well as to his many associates in adult work.

Through nearly three decades the author has enjoyed the friendship of leaders of adults in all the denominations, and with them he continues to have faith in the value of adult Christian education.

EARL F. ZEIGLER

*Philadelphia, Pa.*

7

## ADULTHOOD

Maturing is the criterion of adulthood;
Getting older has little to do with it.

Children and youth endure the first two decades of life, hoping it will be better when they are grown up. Adulthood is their land of promise. People who have entered adulthood, or are far on the route, often have severe spells of nostalgia to return to childhood.

Is there no remedy for keeping human beings satisfied?

A Christian philosophy of life learns about the route that a wise Creator has mapped for his children to follow. A more perfect home life would resolve some of the frustrations that children and youth endure, but even the ideal Christian home cannot protect children and youth from the inevitable tensions of growing, out of which tensions character is created. The purpose of the home is not to avoid experiences that mold character but to guide them to constructive goals.

Age-grading has served a useful purpose in public and church education for children and youth. The biological development of children and youth follows well-charted courses that permit classifications into age group patterns. However, when money and facilities permit, children and youth are not kept rigidly within these patterns, but are given educational opportunities commensurate with their varied capacities.

Adulthood is not a condition that always requires age-grading. For administrative purposes we may be compelled to draw lines that include such terms as young adults, middle-aged adults, older adults. These are conveniences, not rigid requirements. In practice we permit in our churches many combinations of these age groupings for better educational and spiritual development.

## What, Then, Is Adulthood?

Adulthood is growing up, not " grown up." Adults never arrive; they are always arriving. The map of their life is a series of goals to be achieved.

Entrance into adulthood is determined by the demands of life. Adulthood begins when life compels growing persons to accept adult responsibilities. The boy of seventeen or eighteen who is drafted or enlists in the Armed Forces has to be an adult. The girl of seventeen who marries leaps into adulthood at a bound. The young man who is graduated from high school and chooses to enter a vocation instead of going on to college has entered adulthood. If the high school graduate decides to go to college, he may not become an adult immediately upon matriculation, but he is going through a transition stage that is more adult than youth.

Church directors of youth and of adult work have had many an argument over who should carry administrative responsibility for persons in this twilight zone between youth and adulthood. Not so many years ago the dividing line was arbitrarily set so that those under twenty-four would be in the youth bracket and those over twenty-four in the adult bracket. It didn't last long. Many persons married before twenty, the majority before twenty-four. It did seem a bit ridiculous to classify married people as young people, so marriage was made a criterion for entrance into adulthood — at least for church administration purposes. Then came questions like these: If a young person enters upon his vocation, earning his livelihood, has he become an adult? If he enters the Armed Services, should the youth department or the adult department minister to him? These issues and others were resolved in time. In the chapter on young adult work more attention will be given to the decisions that have been reached for a division of responsibility that permits youth directors and adult directors to know where they are going.

In the meantime youth and young adults have not exactly fallen between the cracks.

*Adulthood U.S.A.*

A child born into the present cultural milieu of the U.S.A. is introduced into the most complex situation conceivable. Sociologically he may be classified as higher upper, upper, lower upper; upper middle, middle, lower middle; upper lower, lower, lower lower. Don't laugh; this is serious sociological vocabulary. He may be born Roman Catholic, Protestant, Greek Orthodox, Jewish, or of one of a variety of other religious or nonreligious parentages. His ancestors can be of " pure " strain, going back to the *Mayflower;* or he can be a mixture of nearly all the national and racial groups that have inhabited the earth. His chances of being born Negro, Japanese, Indian, or some other strain are fairly high.

How will all these factors affect his adulthood? Economically and socially he may remain through all or a portion of his childhood and youth in the sociological bracket into which he was born. But this is not at all certain. In the U.S.A., people are constantly moving into the " higher " brackets and some into the " lower." ( " Higher " and " lower " are social criteria, and must not compromise the churches' service for and with people.) Colorwise he will find severe social restrictions, but America is rethinking its attitude and practices on color. Religiously he will have considerable freedom of choice as he approaches adulthood, but again no complete freedom.

We are compelled to admit that the child is to a great extent the father of adulthood in the U.S.A.

When the child enters adulthood and seeks a livelihood, hundreds of vocations are open to both men and women. Less and less this is a man's world. Suffrage is becoming almost universal; grave responsibilities thereby rest on citizenship.

Protestant churches carry the major responsibility for the evangelization and Christian education of adults in the U.S.A. America remains in the mid-twentieth century of a pronounced Protestant complexion. This fact carries no boast or threat to those of a non-Protestant persuasion except to declare that the right of freedom of religious expression will be maintained.

*Beginning Adulthood*

In our culture, early or beginning adulthood is worse than being an adolescent. Granted that teen-agers have been holding the limelight for a long time because of their unpredictable behavior, some of which precipitates serious problems for them and their guardians, the facts of life are that young adults are in a more treacherous stage. A child is age-graded. He knows where he belongs. A nine-year-old in church or public school has status not given to an eight-year-old. And the eight-year-old has superior privileges over his six-year-old brother or sister. Hence, a child keeps striving for the position awaiting him in the next grade. Much the same rule holds for adolescence. Junior and senior high are well-defined states of being, each with special privileges, special responsibilities, and special status.

The time arrives, however, when youth ends and adulthood begins like the crack of dawn. Age-grading has little significance now. The thing that counts is status — a kind of tyrant that rules over much of the world, and has branches of its authority well established in the U.S.A. Society now demands that the young adult act his age. No, that isn't exactly what they mean. Age doesn't count for much. What society means is: You will have to prove that you can go it on your own. We have been subsidizing you for two decades. Now it is your turn to pay back on our investment.

Society may not want to be cruel; there are plenty of resources to aid the young adult in getting started; nevertheless, he has an ambition to show what he can do. And this is all to the good.

Beginning adulthood usually includes before long three major experiences that are new: getting married, adjusting to married life, having a baby. It takes two to get married, two to make adjustment, two to have a baby. Hence, husband and wife, both young adults, are thrust into these new experiences, often without adequate preparation, or without knowledge of where to obtain competent advice. Things are getting better with the growth of courses in preparation for marriage; marriage counseling; and prenatal clinics for expectant mothers and fathers.

Presumably, the choice of an occupation has preceded marriage and the beginning of a family. Even so, the young adult may soon discover that he is not quite settled in his vocation, and may feel the need of shopping around to get what he thinks he needs to maintain the mythical status he desires. Usually, he has gone into debt to buy a home, or if he rents, to furnish his living quarters with the style of furnishings that his status demands. Keeping up with proverbial Joneses is another tyrant he has to pay homage to. New social responsibilities make life a merry-go-round. Some of these social activities may demand a compromise with his earlier standards of conduct, thus creating a spiritual problem.

If church and school training have challenged the growing adolescent to accept citizenship and religious responsibilities, the increasing pressures of married life, social obligations, and vocational success tend to postpone and dull his sensibilities on these matters. And if his vocation requires mobility, either as a salesman, or because he must move to a new location, community roots do not go deep. There is a constant tug of war for his time, money, and abilities.

The church may or may not reach him at this stage of his adulthood. If he can be enlisted in the worship and organized life of the church, there is strong probability that he will be mightily helped in making the many adjustments so necessary to integrating his life around Christian living. How necessary that the church have a program well conceived and executed to meet the interests and needs of these valuable people!

By this time the reader is raising the question about young adults who do not marry early, or who continue single. They surely have many of the problems already hinted at, and some not referred to. If marriage is desired, and no suitable mate can be found, there may be frustrations commensurate with those of the married, but of a different nature. These people, too, need the counsel and fellowship of church groups to enable them to resolve their problems in the light of the gospel of Christ.

This is not the chapter to go into detail on a church program for young adulthood. That will be reserved until later.

## Continuing Adulthood

Again, it should be said that middle adulthood is not adequately described by calling these people an " age group." For chronological purposes middle adulthood covers the ages from thirty or thirty-five up to sixty or sixty-five. Within this range can be included the majority of adults who have married and are rearing families. If marriage occurred in the early twenties, and children followed in due succession — a family of four children, let us surmise — by the age of fifty the parents have been responsible for rearing offspring who are now twenty and more years of age. The first-born are themselves getting married and starting the life cycle anew. The youngest child is probably still in college, and the drain on the family budget is lightening but not completely liquidated.

The experiences through which this family have wended their way have made life a continuous adventure in sharing, worrying, adjusting, and achieving. If reasonably successful, all can join in a glad *Te Deum.* Along the route the father has been a husband, wage earner, family provider, co-operative homemaker, citizen, churchman, and may have become quite a man of affairs. The mother has been a wife, family adviser and manager, and has participated in all kinds of church and community activities. If she has recognized the potentialities of spiritual maturing, she has grown with the years and with her arduous responsibilities. She has taken the inevitable biological changes in her stride, and is prepared to enter older adulthood with confidence and poise.

What we have been describing is middle-aged parenthood that has been reasonably successful. It does not always come out so well. Catastrophes, such as divorce, serious illness, death of one of the family, failure of one or more of the children, do occur with such frequency that they cannot be disregarded. The cold statistics of family failures stare the church and social agencies right in the face.

Whether the participants in middle adulthood are married or single, they are confronted with the complex problems of citizenship responsibilities, churchmanship, a standard of living, what to do with leisure time, how to adjust to biological changes that can be ameliorated but not avoided. Married couples must also face up to each other's peculiar needs. They are not so young, sometimes not so attractive, as they used to be. Compensations are a must. There is nothing more pleasurable to behold than a couple keeping in love all through middle adulthood. It doesn't always happen, the records sadly declare. It could happen more often if the church program of adult Christian education were timed and tuned to offer resources to these people.

Later in this volume suggestions will be given to describe a church program for middle adulthood that contains the promise of strengthening those families which are courageously plowing forward, of giving better assistance to those who are failing, and of ministering to the married or unmarried who comprise this fascinating sector of society.

### Arriving Adulthood

Sudden popularity has come to older adults, senior citizens, or whatever we choose to call them. Books, magazines, pamphlets, movies, TV, medical profession, churches, social agencies, foundations, life-insurance companies, industry, legislatures, Congress — have we omitted

anything?—have all climbed on the band
claim the worth of older people. They are on to pro-
ing lionized and flattered to their spoilation ger of be-

This is purposely overdrawn to emphasize
tual situation with hundreds of thousands of o. the ac-
demands more rather than less of everything tha people
done at present for assisting and enlisting them being
urgent needs. They are constantly *aging*, but a m heir
are *aged*. The aging that began at birth is continui ity
spiritual destiny. To resist or resent this process is to qu ts
tion a wise Creator's purpose. Death, the inevitable closing
door to aging, is as much a part of God's plan as birth.

We like to call older adulthood *arriving* adulthood because it is the last of life for which the first was made. This
era of arriving adulthood may last ten, twenty, thirty or
more years. Actuarial projections are being changed constantly because life expectancy is increasing. Men and
women who have reached sixty-five in reasonable repair
should plan to live an additional ten or eleven years at the
least. Since this is the average expectancy, a large number
will live much longer than that.

Our concern with older people in this initial chapter is
to recognize them as belonging to the maturing experience
we call adulthood. They are a part of and not apart from
the whole range of adulthood that began in the twenties,
or earlier. They belong to the school of life that never dis-
misses its pupils by "graduation." Continued learning is
not only an older adult's opportunity; it is his necessity.

The American way of life no longer condones using people up as rapidly as possible because the supply is limitless
and the scrap heap a ready means of disposal. If we ever
thought that way about our natural resources, we now
conserve them by better methods of processing, and by
replenishing them where that is possible, for example, by

forests. But human beings are more than nat-
growin s, and they need never become parasites if so-
ural re rganize to allow their productive powers to
ciety

conti urch contains a high proportion of older people
in lowship. But are they really in the fellowship? To
be ame on the roll; to be an appointment for a visit on
th astor's cluttered date book; to be a listener with or
out a hearing aid — are these the ends for which men
d women of older years are destined?

Churches that are alert to the potentialities of all their
constituency are not satisfied to see older people dwarfed
into insignificance by failure to enlist them in their own
spiritual maturing, and in utilizing them to contribute to
others. If living long has built up a reservoir of experience
that contains the riches of life, then the church must permit that reservoir of power to flow into other lives. One of
the bright spots in the church firmament is the recognition
that older people are useful people, and that they must be
used. To use them, some of the same procedures that are
applied to other areas of church work must be attempted:
surveys to know the facts about older people in the congregation; their enlistment in organizations and in corporate worship; provision for meeting learning needs; but
above all, an understanding attitude that draws older people into the core of fellowship.

Older people must be encouraged not only to see themselves as others see them, but to examine themselves criti-
cally in the light of the new knowledge that is rapidly becoming available from gerontologists and geriatricians;
from sociologists and psychologists; from economists and
legislators; and also from church leaders. These older people must learn to face reality. Occupationally, the majority
of them must retire. Biologically, adjustments have to be

made to bodily changes and needs. Socially, new outlets must be discovered and used. In housing and food, other changes become a must. Economically, living costs and, for the majority, reduced income require careful planning. Educationally, learning needs can be satisfied with all the facilities that society is providing, almost lavishly. Spiritually, this period of life should be the most satisfying of all. Even though all these adjustments have to be made, they can become the challenging forces to provide older people with incentives to live to the full.

A favorite Bible quotation for every older person might be, " No one who puts his hand to the plow and looks back is fit for the kingdom of God." — Luke 9:62.

Others might prefer Paul's magnificent philosophy of life, " One thing I do, forgetting what lies behind and straining forward to what lies ahead, I press on toward the goal for the prize of the upward call of God in Christ Jesus." — Phil. 3:13-14.

In a later chapter more detailed information will be provided for organizing and promoting adult Christian education with and for older people. It is a promising outlook as several denominations have already discovered.

## Implications for Christian Education

1. *Adulthood is the longest period of living, lasting at the present life expectancy for fifty years or more.* Childhood and youth are the opening doors to the vast vistas beyond. The church program of Christian education must help children and youth to be introduced to the rich heritage of the faith, and capitalize on it for their own growing needs. Then adult education must take over and provide a program that will be lifelong. There is no alternative.

2. *All periods of adulthood are probably equally im-*

*portant.* Beginning adulthood may seem more glamorous, continuing adulthood more achieving, and expectant arriving adulthood more uncertain; but Christian education has a stake in all these periods and its program must be continuous and efficient.

3. *The culture in which adulthood is maturing contains both assets and liabilities.* Adults must learn to appraise the culture and help to change its climate so that their spiritual maturing may have sure direction. To this task Christian education must devote intelligence to assure that its program is beamed to the age in which we live for the ends to which we are born.

## WHAT IS ADULT CHRISTIAN EDUCATION?

Adult Christian education is the enlistment and guidance
of adults in their own spiritual maturing.

Education, like aging, begins at birth and continues to
the end of life. It may be good education or poor education, just as there can be desirable and undesirable aging.
But as aging is going on all the time from birth until death,
so education must be a continuous process.

There is no end to learning as long as there is life. If
learning stops before death, life shrivels and becomes a
burden. The prime method of handling the burdens of life
is to keep on learning how to live, that is, how to age as
symmetrically as possible.

Another way to describe adult Christian education is to
call it the means of aging spiritually. But that word " aging " has a sinister sound to many who have not fathomed
its spiritual significance. Aging is something every human
being must accomplish to achieve the purpose for which
he was created by God. It is not a milestone in life that is
reached at sixty or seventy; aging began with emergence
from the womb, and is God's appointed process for maturing.

Aging, therefore, should be growing toward maturity.
But maturity itself is a process. We do better to speak of
*maturing* rather than *maturity*. For children we try to provide the means of their aging so that they grow biologically, psychologically, and spiritually into maturing childhood. For youth the same general provisions are made, but

we recognize that biological maturing transforms youth into fitness for accomplishing the purposes of adulthood. Once adulthood is reached, maturing must continue because the needs and interests of adulthood require continuing adaptation to the demands of a complex life.

Once we are born we must start aging. There is no turning back from life without losing it. When education and aging keep pace with each other, life develops symmetrically. The goal of every Christian may be worded in what Luke wrote about the child of Nazareth: "And Jesus increased in wisdom and in stature, and in favor with God and man."

## Correlation and Co-operation for Adult Education

In the local church the adult men and women are the candidates for adult education. To reach and enlist them in their own spiritual maturing — their spiritual aging — must be the concern of adult work, men's work, women's work, mission and educational boards, and any other administrative units responsible for adults. The adult is a unit; the approach to him and his needs must be as unified as possible.

National agencies realize the necessity of a unified approach. More and more through the years they have created interlocking committees that share plans and programs that have a common aim.

Correlation and co-operation at the national level must be the rule also at the local church level. Men's work and women's work in the local church may be related administratively to a different agency than the adult study group. The worshiping congregation is administered by the pastor and church officers. But adults in the local church are members of these different groupings, and they must see unity in these educational programs if they are to achieve unity in their spiritual maturing.

How to bring unified effort into all these apparently divergent interests will be one of the purposes of this book as its chapters develop. There will be nothing really new to suggest; rather, out of all that the different denominations are doing will be listed those things that are bringing results in adult Christian education. The last three or four decades have taught adult leaders many things that they can do, and some things that they cannot and should not do. Their experiences now become our guidance for planning the future of adult Christian education.

## Biblical Foundations of Adult Christian Education

One of the oft-neglected emphases in adult Christian education is the recognition that theology is essential to Christian education. It used to be popular to encourge laymen to say, " No theology for me; leave that to the preacher; give me practical Christianity." And the joker was that pastors and leaders of adults fell for this fallacy. For a fallacy it is. There can be no sound Christian education, including adult education, that does not rest on sound theology.

And what is theology? It is the word about God, speaking etymologically. It is the revealed word of God to be applied to the needs of our aging — to our spiritual maturing.

The Apostles' Creed and the Nicene Creed are theology. Through these creeds we confess our faith, and affirm for ourselves what our forebears in the faith discovered through trial and error, through conflict and persecution.

The Biblical doctrine of man, his sin, provision for his redemption, and the work of Christ and the Holy Spirit in the redeeming process are all theological convictions.

The doctrine of the church has to be understood theologically before it can enter into our adult Christian education. To try to make good Christians out of church members without helping them to understand the nature, order, and nurture of the church is like trying to make bricks without straw.

Likewise, the practical aspects of Christianity, as we have been inclined to dub them, all have a theological foundation, or they do not fit into the Christian ethic. We cannot have Christian teaching on citizenship that will stand up under fire unless it is grounded in the prophets and the ethic of Jesus and the apostolic teaching.

Our need in adult Christian education is for more theology, not less. However, we would not insist that lay leaders of adults must be " experts " in theology before they receive certificates to teach. Leaders are learners whose theology should grow with their own spiritual maturing.

## Philosophy of Adult Christian Education

Underlying adult Christian education is the philosophy of all education, the ability of human beings to learn. They are not the victims of a closed system of instincts or natural behavior, however valuable that may be for a nonhuman animal. Birds build their nests after their own kind as they have been doing for centuries. Man has to learn to build his dwellings. Nonhuman animals, many of them, develop rapidly and can reproduce their kind quickly. The human animal must develop through a slow process. This is his greatest asset because it makes education or learning possible.

We need not labor this point except to say that the aging process in human beings is matched constantly by learning ability. This ability never wears out. Ample experiments are on record to prove that the learning ability of adults is equal to all their needs. If we believe this demonstrated fact, we shall never doubt the worth of adult education. Rather, we shall use it more intelligently to make adulthood the crowning glory of aging.

This philosophy of education includes what we have discovered about the way human beings learn. There are established laws of learning known and recognized by all engaged in the education of children and youth, and these same laws serve the interests and needs of adults.

Developmental psychology is describing the learning process as response to tasks that must be undertaken when the growing person is ready. Each period of aging requires response to the tasks normative to that period, and as the person responds learning takes place. A child who would not try to walk or talk in early childhood, if the ability to learn were present, would pass into the next stage of aging severely handicapped. Educators are using a term that challenges leaders and learners — the *teachable moment*, when learning can occur most rapidly and efficiently. As aging progresses, tasks of many varieties challenge the person to master them. Thus from birth to death these teachable moments occur, and wise is the teacher who knows when the opportunity has arrived. Wise also is the learner who knows how to enlist his powers in the learning process.

Our efforts at adult Christian education are hampered often by the failure of persons to have learned what they should have in their earlier aging. But the case is not hopeless. Adults can learn what they failed earlier to master; thus they can catch up on themselves.

Another liability for adult education is the inability of many to understand their own needs. They do not respond when the teachable moment has come. Quite as often their leaders do not recognize these adult needs, and the big opportunity slips away. If the teachable moment has come in an adult group, and the leader insists on giving them the " lesson " he has prepared regardless, he may think he is doing his duty by the lesson course, but he is not doing his duty to the group, which should be his primary concern.

A further obstacle in adult Christian learning is the fact of sin. To ignore this element in human nature is to falsify the facts of life. Sin possesses the saint as well as the depraved individual. All are in need of forgiveness. Sin sets up barriers to God's educating processes because the sinner is a rebel who withstands discipline. One teachable moment after another may come, but if the potential learner resists what God is trying to break through and do with him, even the finest methods and leadership are in vain. Adult Christian education is based on the thesis that the learner has to be enlisted and guided in his own spiritual maturing. When sin prevents his enlistment, it has to be overcome before learning can take place. The repentant and contrite heart is the beginning and continuation of wisdom. No doubt many groups of adults are slowed down constantly by the unwillingness of the members to be submissive to God, be forgiven of their sins, and open their minds and hearts to the inflowing wisdom from on high.

## The Individual and the Group

The word " individual " is more or less of a misnomer — more rather than less, we should assume. Every individual, so-called, is the product of parents and grandparents, and forebears without number. He is an omnibus in which all his ancestors ride. To call him an individual is just to say that he is different from all others who have preceded him and who will follow him.

His ancestry, his biological inheritance, provided him with a capital with which to begin aging and maturing. Every time he learns, his capital is being invested to produce what God intended him to be.

This individual, so-called, is born into a culture. Sometimes it is pagan, sometimes Christian, but his culture provides the opportunities for making him what he will become. Christian education attempts to overcome the antagonistic forces of his culture by teaching the Christian principles and practices. Thus, it is possible for a child, a youth, or an adult to live in a culture that is not conducive to Christian personality and still be a Christian. The early followers of Jesus accomplished this feat, and we go back to their record to supply a great deal of the teaching material that we use in our churches. In the Old Testament we use the records of the Hebrews who were a chosen people of God to combat the pull of surrounding cultures and become a witness to God's eternal purpose for mankind.

Without the group reinforcement neither the ancient Hebrews nor the followers of Jesus would have been very successful. They achieved because they learned in a group to draw upon resources outside themselves for their own reinforcement of purpose. Among the Hebrews the family was a strong supporting group. Among the early followers of Jesus both the family and the fellowship of believers — a minority group at first — were the strengthening influences.

This idea leads to a consideration of what is probably the most important fact for adult Christian education. It is the educating influence of the group.

## The Fellowship or Koinōnia

Fellowship is a term that Americans apply to almost any and every kind of grouping. There must be a tremendous appeal to the idea or we would not use it so much. There must be in human nature a longing for fellowship that nothing but a group can supply.

Proponents of adult education, both secular and Christian, have known from the beginning that fellowship was the climate in which best learning could take place. That is why group procedures have multiplied so rapidly. Each new method was an effort to utilize the fellowship group to bring out the best that was in each of the members. Take the familiar Philipps 66, or buzz method. What is this but enlarging the opportunities in a group for every member to take part as a participant and a contributor? Reticent members who would not have the courage to speak before a large group find their voices, and express their ideas, when five or six are huddled together. Thus, growth can take place and, in time, the shy member may develop word power as well as idea expression.

The Christian church has been working with this educational power of the fellowship group since its origin. In fact many modern interpreters of the New Testament are bold to say that the fellowship group, or *koinōnia,* was the matrix out of which the church emerged.

It is interesting to observe that the author of The Acts seems to lack a terminology to describe what occurred at Pentecost and following to produce a body of believers who did not exist previously. In Acts 2:41, Luke is trying to describe the tremendous response to Peter's sermon under the power of the Holy Spirit. Luke says, " There were added that day about three thousand souls." Added to what? Luke had no name for the phenomenon. But in v. 42 he coins a word that seems to fit the situation, " And they devoted themselves to the apostle's teaching and fellowship ( *koinōnia* )."

This *koinōnia* is a New Testament phenomenon that can

be accounted for only as we accept the work of the Holy
Spirit to produce it. It seems to have sprung into existence
almost instantaneously. It was composed of a varied as-
sortment of principally Jewish adherents who had been
so convicted by Peter's sermon that they had cried out to
him and the other apostles, " Brethren, what shall we do? "
And Peter had told them to repent, to be baptized, and
they would receive the Holy Spirit. Their response had
been the signal for the Holy Spirit's empowering of them
to become a *koinōnia.*

The idea of this kind of fellowship for adult Christian
education is too good to leave as a museum piece of New
Testament history. It has immediate possibilities for every
kind of group or organization that we have created, or will
create in our modern churches. Wherever adults group
themselves for study, for action, for worship, for recreation, for administration, there is the opportunity to produce
a fellowship — a *koinōnia.* Church officers can work to this
end as they meet to administer their part of the church's
business and program. Every adult study class can seek
to become a *koinōnia.* So can men's organizations and
women's organizations. And the worshiping congregation
is a natural to become a *koinōnia.* If this is worthy of striving for in the local church, it must also be the goal toward which all overhead organizations direct their delib-
erations.

Lest we try to induce *koinōnia* by clever maneuvering of
groups, we should always curb such unholy desires by re-
membering that the source of *koinōnia* is the Holy Spirit.
He is the much neglected Agent in our adult educational
program. We have become skillful in role-playing, discussion, panels, brain-storming, lectures, symposium, forum,
and a dozen other techniques. We have bowed down to
the worship of group dynamics. But if we have kept the

Holy Spirit waiting at the door, we have toiled in vain.

The fellowship called *koinōnia* is the strongest force we know in education to weld people into a unity, not a uniformity. If God had wanted uniformity, he would have made all of us to look much alike, to think alike, to behave alike. He must love variety because he has not made any two of us to be alike. It is this unlikeness in unity that creates the best climate we know anything about for adult learning to take place. Here the strong bear the burdens of the weak. Those who know much share with those who know less. The man with more to give gains when he gives; and the man with little to give also grows when he shares. Here people with variant views get them tested in the crucible of discussion. The gold is refined of its dross. The timid are encouraged; the extroverts are taught to behave. Long ago Paul put the idea we are trying to express in unforgettable words: " Each is given the manifestation of the Spirit for the common good." — I Cor. 12:7.

From the Section on Evangelism of the 1954 Evanston Assembly came this excellent statement about the church as a fellowship. It applies equally to the church's program of adult education.

" The church which God uses to communicate the gospel is a fellowship, a *koinōnia,* drawn and held together by the love of Christ through the power of the Holy Spirit and by the need and desire of its members to share this experience with each other and to draw those outside into that *koinōnia.* The evangelizing church will offer this gift in its preaching and teaching; in its acts of worship and administration of its sacraments; through the individual and group witness of its members; by leading its people to base their life upon God's Word used in personal and family devotions; by fostering small fellowships; and by works of social service."

## IMPLICATIONS FOR ADULT WORK

1. *Adult Christian education is enlistment and guidance.*
The ancient saw that " you can't teach an old dog new
tricks " isn't so. Adults aren't old dogs. Furthermore, you
can teach a dog what he wants to be taught if the teacher
knows more than the dog, and knows how to handle dogs.
Enlistment and guidance of adults in their own spiritual
maturing is partly their decision, but not entirely. Leaders
must show the values to be gained by growing toward the
prize of the high calling of God in Christ Jesus.

2. *Adult education assures more competent leadership
for the education of children and youth.* Until parents continue their own education, their children are denied the
guidance to which they are entitled. Surveys have conclusively shown that the home, for good or for ill, is the
most potent force in molding the character of the child.
Likewise, those adults who plan the program for children
and youth must be growing persons themselves.

3. *Christian living is the goal of adult education.* Since
the gospel created the church, it must be the gospel that
the church proclaims in all its ministries.

4. *Every organization that enrolls adults must become
an adult educator.* Because organizations provide opportunities for more intimate associations, they can become the
*koinōnia* that is so essential for the Spirit's guidance for
learning the Christian way.

5. *The Holy Spirit is the essential agent in Christian
education.* He makes available all the means of grace by
which people grow spiritually. He produces the fellowship; convicts of sin; gives peace through repentance and
forgiveness; guides and disciplines the growing Christian;
and helps the learner to achieve the great gift of God —
the life of righteousness.

## ADULT INTERESTS AND NEEDS

*Interests and needs are the raw materials for enlist-
ing men and women in their own spiritual maturing.*

How to enlist men and women in a program of Christian education designed for their own spiritual maturing
generates plenty of frustrations for their leaders (and probably for the men and women themselves).

A sincere pastor who was participating in a leadership
seminar expressed the feeling of many in the group when
he remarked: "I am trying to teach an adult class. If I
give them what I think they *need*, they show little *interest*.
But if I teach what interests them, I feel that I have com-
promised my commission."

Unwittingly, perhaps, the pastor was voicing what has
long plagued our efforts in Christian education, namely,
that if a thing is interesting, really interesting, does it
thereby lack some religious essential? The extreme of this
point of view would be, "Religion cannot be palatable; it
must have a bitter taste to be efficacious." (Some people
still believe that bitter medicine has more potency than the
tasty kind.)

At the other extreme are misguided leaders who try so
hard to make religion interesting that they never reach
the deeper needs of learners.

If neither of these views is sound education, we must
discover how to resolve the problem of interests and needs,
because both of them are necessary and relevant for enlisting men and women in their own spiritual maturing. Let

us pursue a few questions that are pertinent to this exploration.

## What Is the Relation Between Interests and Needs?

An interest may be described as anything that produces a feeling of wanting to know more about a thing, or wanting to see it; or do something about it; or own it, or share it; or take part in it. An interest has the power to arouse these kinds of feelings.

A need is simply a useful or desired thing that is lacking. It may be strongly desired, in which case the learner is willing to put forth an effort to supply the lack. The young man who came to Jesus with the question, " Good Teacher, what shall I do to inherit eternal life? " thought he had an intense interest in that subject. When Jesus told him the requirements for eternal life, and the young man replied, " All these I have observed; what do I still lack? " he was told to do something that he had probably never thought of as related to eternal life. When he went away sorrowful he was admitting that his interest in eternal life was insufficient to make him pay the price of meeting his lack — of meeting his real need.

Interests and needs may run into competition, as they often do.

Contrast the refusal of the young man with the case of Peter's taking a nap on the housetop of Simon the tanner in Joppa. The vision of clean and unclean animals that so perplexed Peter was an indication that already he had felt a strong interest in the conversion of the Gentiles. But he had not permitted that interest to thrust him into intimate contact with non-Jews. He may have felt more or less strongly at times that this was a need to be met by the gospel. The clash of interests and needs persisted until Peter was called downstairs to confront immediate need in the person of non-Jews who implored him to come to Caesarea to explain the gospel to Cornelius.

In that moment Peter realized his *lack*. To be an apostle of Jesus Christ he must not be partial with the gospel. Since God had no partiality toward non-Jews, Peter must share the gospel with them.

He did not go away sorrowful; he went with glad willingness, and the household of Cornelius received the good news.

### Are All Adult Interests Assets of Religious Significance?

To list all the interests of adults would be an endless task. We would have to list the interests that develop as a person continues to age, as well as those that belong to vocations, recreations, avocations and hobbies, and a multitude of other areas.

Our concern is whether any and all the interests of adults have religious significance, that is, can Christian education utilize the variety of adult interests to help men and women in their spiritual maturing?

Take the man who loves golf and is so interested in it that he will devote almost every spare hour to improving his score. From a religious angle golf is a commendable form of recreation. But when the golfer absents himself from an adult study group on Sunday, or rationalizes his nonattendance at corporate worship by quipping that " A man can worship God in the open on Sunday on a golf course," there is a valid question whether the golfer is not permitting his love of the game to be an alibi for his obligations to God, family, and the church.

Or take the man who is advancing in his profession. There is no doubt of his interest in his work. He is fitted for it; he is growing in competence; and he is maintaining a high level of ethics in all that he does. But to carry the load, he has to cut corners in his religious obligations. He has no time, so he says, to teach a class of boys, or to accept office in the church; and he is absent more often than present from corporate worship.

For both the golfer and the professional man the problem is to guide their respective interests so that they do not compete with their religious needs. Both these men have religious needs that cannot be completely supplied with golf or profession. If the golfer can meet his recreational, physical, and social needs in golfing, as he has a right to, then as a follower of Christ he has to be challenged to meet his religious needs by giving honest consideration to the claims of Christ. The zeal that he shows for golf is a quality of zeal that may be very useful in religious work. Likewise, the professional man with his tremendous vocational drive has something that can be dedicated to Kingdom work.

We face a different problem when we deal with men and women whose interests carry them far afield from religion. They develop a way of life that virtually destroys their powers to become interested in the program of the church. They give their time and money to a round of activities that the church cannot approve — drinking, gambling, loose living, philandering, and wasting their substance on that which neither edifies nor assists others in the fight for character. These people have plenty of interests — that we must admit. The rub is that their interests are in conflict with their spiritual needs, and there is little hope of enlisting them in their own spiritual maturing until they can be brought to acknowledge and admit that their interests are detrimental to their welfare and the good of others.

Some men and women who fall into the category just described may still be carried on a church roll. They become the "problem children" for the church to reclaim.

And adult Christian education has to be concerned with their redemption. Fortunately, we hope, the majority of such men and women are not on church rolls. Thus they become the outreach of the church in its program of evangelism.

All this seems to add up to the conclusion that adult interests, by and large, are potential assets for Christian education. If they are not, if these interests are antireligious, then the task is to change the " anti " into the positive.

*What Are the Needs of Growing Men and Women?*

Those engaged professionally in adult Christian education believe that they know what adults *need* for their spiritual growth. The trick is to get the co-operation of adults in their own recognition of *felt* needs.

Until a need is felt, it remains in hibernation, or as a seed that has not yet germinated. But this is not the whole story. Needs also operate on a time schedule. A young married couple has needs that an octogenarian may have once had but no longer finds necessary to consider. Similarly, an older adult develops needs that young adults know nothing about.

These obvious facts compel adult Christian education to include in its program an extensive reservoir of resources upon which to draw for ministering to men and women who enter adulthood in their twenties (or even younger) and continue in the state of adulthood until the sun of life has set. These long-lived adults are in every conceivable category: married, single, widowed, divorced; married with children, without children, with grandparents; in all kinds of vocations and avocations; sick and well; churched and unchurched; social-minded, antisocial, inactive in social affairs; educated and uneducated; spiritually maturing, arrested in development, headed backward;

leaders, followers; aggressive, indifferent, hostile; co-operative, non-co-operative. To extend the listing is merely to
illustrate how complex adulthood is. If we shudder at the
task of guiding youth into a satisfying Christian experience, we do well to stand in awe before the problem of
enlisting men and women in the gospel program.

If there is a way to help men and women recognize their
needs when the opportunity is ripe, and understand these
as *felt* needs, then we can have some hope of releasing the
redemptive forces.

The demands of the gospel determine the needs of men
and women. They can fit themselves to participate fully in
the gospel program.

## How Does the Gospel Program Match Adult Needs?

Is it unwarranted dogmatism to affirm that the gospel
taught and lived by Jesus Christ was designed carefully to
match and meet adult needs? Jesus declared his conviction in such a sweeping statement as, " I am the way, and
the truth, and the life." — John 14:6.

This brings us to the theological implications of adult
Christian education. We must study Bible teaching carefully to know what it has to offer for meeting our needs.
The Sermon on the Mount, for example, covers a wide
range of divine resources for human needs. Beginning with
the Beatitudes, we find not only a listing of several human
needs but the resources for ministering to these lacks.
Needs mentioned are:

humbleness in spirit
ability to mourn
meekness
hunger and thirst for righteousness
merciful attitudes and practices
pureness of heart

peacemaking attitudes and practices
ability to stand up under persecution
ability to rejoice

Would anyone who makes a pretense of understanding
adults refuse to admit that every one of these in the list
represents a pressing human need? I need to develop a
spirit that is *poor* so that I can appropriate the riches that
God offers in Kingdom living. I need to be *merciful,* not
to obtain the reward of having others extend mercy to me,
but to enter into and identify myself with another's strug-
gles, sorrows, and aspirations.

Profitable time could be spent by an adult study group
in identifying and listing all the needs referred to in just
one small area of the Bible like the Sermon on the Mount.
Further listing could then be made of other portions of the
Bible. This procedure would convince adults that the Bible
does cover the whole sweep of human needs, as well as
provide the resources for supplying human lacks. It would
also help to uncover the theological foundations on which
Christian education must build. Certainly we have no
right to attempt to build on any other foundation than is
already laid — the foundation of Jesus Christ.

Difficulty is often encountered in identifying a need
mentioned in the Bible with a felt need of a contemporary
adult. It is reported that in one vocational retreat of farm-
ers held for spiritual enrichment, a member of the group
asked the leader, " Will you describe the Christian way to
sell a kicking cow to a neighbor who needs a cow but
would not necessarily need a cantankerous beast such as I
own? " Obviously none of the group recalled a reference in
the Bible to a kicking cow. After the laughter had run its
course, the leader asked the group for their opinion. One
replied instantly that he thought the Golden Rule covered

this case adequately, even though it said nothing about a kicking cow. Another took a Bible and began to search diligently. Soon he came up with an exhibit from Ex. 21: 28–32, where it describes the ancient Hebrew law for adjusting difficulties when an ox has gored a man or woman, especially when it was known that the ox had a reputation for beastly behavior. The group were convinced that the Bible was more comprehensive than they had known or imagined.

There are times, however, when the Bible does not have the spelled-out answers to pressing human need. Does the Bible tell Christians how to vote, and for whom to vote? Does it list the rules for settling racial issues? Does it mention automation? Does it lay down specifics for living in a democracy?

These and many other similar perplexities have not been side-stepped by theologians, educators, and Bible interpreters. They frankly recognize that Christian guidance is needed, and that the Bible's relevance must be demonstrated. Especially is this needed as the ecumenical movement grows. The Bible speaks to all denominations, and it must have a sure word that all can recognize. On the great social issues there must be agreement on what the Bible speaks between Baptist and Presbyterian, Greek Orthodox and Episcopalian. As their leaders sit down together to study a particular passage of the Bible, it is thrilling to learn that their minds begin to flow in the same channels under the guidance of the Holy Spirit.

As Christians, we continue to believe that God speaks through his Holy Spirit to the situation facing us, when we respond in obedience and love.

By no means is this a proof-text method of Biblical interpretation; it is, however, using the Bible to permit the Holy Spirit to do what Jesus promised he would: " But the

Counselor, the Holy Spirit, whom the Father will send in my name, he will teach you all things, and bring to your remembrance all that I have said to you." — John 14:26.

Couple this with our risen Lord's statement to two men on the road to Emmaus: " O foolish men, and slow of heart to believe all that the prophets have spoken! Was it not necessary that the Christ should suffer these things and enter into his glory? "

Then we are told: " And beginning with Moses and all the prophets, he interpreted to them in all the scriptures the things concerning himself." — Luke 24:25–27.

Before we leave this subject of needs we are compelled to face up to what theologians are calling a " predicament." World conditions are so complex that the combined efforts of well-intentioned men and nations cannot extricate them from some of their predicaments. They recognize their needs but they cannot resolve their predicaments. For example, students of racial problems admit that Christians, individually and in groups, may achieve an attitude and a spirit of love that enables them to rise above hatreds, prejudices, and blind spots. Laws may be passed that remove all legal barriers to minority groups. But the task of implementing brotherhood and justice for all still remains unfinished.

The majority of world powers have signed a Universal Declaration of Human Rights. It is a noble statement. How long will it take the world to grant human rights to all its inhabitants. This is just another of our unresolvable predicaments

Our hope is in a God who is also in a " predicament " by having granted man free will and the power of choice. (We are speaking rhetorically, not theologically, just now.) It would be better to say that man's predicament is God's opportunity, and that God's " predicament " is the demonstration of his love, which provides man with opportunities to respond to God's confidence in him.

None of the nonhuman creatures are in predicaments. Man is, because he was created in the image of God.

Thus we have to conclude, sorrowfully, that there are some needs of modern man that cannot be satisfied fully by our program of Christian education. We shall not despair because of this. Constantly we shall be striving, with the help of the Holy Spirit, to let him speak to us in our particular situations, to comfort us in our predicaments, and to lead us onward toward the light.

We shall continue to believe that Christian faith is not static. It is not formulas, easily worked out, nor sets of rules readily applied. Christian faith is life with God, as we respond to his redeeming love revealed in Christ, and made available to us through the Holy Spirit. We shall admit that man cannot save himself, and that the procedures of Christian education will not guarantee Christian conduct. God in Christ is the Savior. Nevertheless, we shall utilize every insight and discipline that human search uncovers in philosophy, psychology, history, and elsewhere that gives us new facets of truth to aid us in understanding more perfectly what God has revealed and is revealing.

Dare we not believe that the Holy Spirit can use all these disciplines, and work through them to lead us forward in our sonship with the Father? Our redemption as individuals must be accompanied by changes in our institutions that bring them under this mighty redemptive process.

" Beloved, we are God's children now; it does not yet appear what we shall be, but we know that when he appears we shall be like him, for we shall see him as he is. And every one who thus hopes in him purifies himself as he is pure." — I John 3:2–3.

*Procedures for Identifying Adult Interests and Needs*

Every local church program already includes numerous resources for meeting adult interests and needs. But the program demands continuing evaluation to assure help to the largest number. Church adults are notorious for taking the line of least resistance so as to " get by " with a minimum of investment of their time and effort. Many are willing to settle for a B or C record of attendance at morning corporate worship, padded with a few additional special meetings. Without minimizing the value of corporate worship, which should be the most important activity in which adults participate, other group activities are also essential for spiritual maturing. To enlist adults in a more comprehensive program is the goal of all local churches. Various procedures have been tested to accomplish this purpose, a sampling of which will be mentioned briefly.

1. *Interest finders.* These can be homemade or secured from denominational or interdenominational sources. They are check lists, mimeographed or printed, on which adults can register their interests. Sometimes these are organized into areas such as: Bible study, theology, church history, family life, vocational problems, national and international affairs, social education and action, leadership, and so forth. Analysis and collation of the checks provide help in determining improvement of the ongoing program.

2. *Observing individuals in group meetings.* An alert leader becomes acquainted quickly with the interests and needs of his group as he watches their reactions in the group proceedings. For best results the group needs an inconspicuous *observer* who possesses a check-list sheet with the names of the group members. At each meeting the observer or the leader keeps a record of significant reactions of individuals. The observer's check list might look something like the evaluation chart on the opposite page.

### EVALUATION OF GROUP PARTICIPATION

| REACTIONS | A | B | C | D | E | F | G | H | I | J | K | L | M | N | O | |
|---|---|---|---|---|---|---|---|---|---|---|---|---|---|---|---|---|
| Asked pertinent questions | × | | | × | | | × | | | | | | | | | |
| Lost his temper when antagonized | | | × | | | | | | | | | | | | | |
| Mediated a dispute | | | | | × | | | | | | | | | | | |
| Belittled a member of the group | | | × | | | | | | | | | | | | | |
| Disagreed violently with leader | | | × | | | | | | | | | | | | × | |
| Helped analyze the problem | | | | | | | | | × | | × | | | | | |
| Led in prayer | | | | × | | | | | | | | | | × | | |
| Talked too much | | × | | | | | | | | | | | | | | |
| Said nothing | | | | | | | × | | × | | × | × | | | | |
| Contributed from personal experience | | | | | | | | | | | | | | | × | |

(NAMES OF MEMBERS)

Obviously this procedure has dangers because it may seem to be a form of spying. Its possibilities are enormous for locating interests and needs, and also for improving group procedures. Both leader and group grow when some form of evaluation like this is used.

3. *Group evaluation of itself.* A group that is seeking to become a fellowship — a *koinōnia* — must learn to check up on itself from time to time. The leader will have his own evaluation check list, both for helping him to look at his own interests and needs, and to appraise his leadership. Then, as members of the group grow into higher levels of fellowship, they, too, will want to learn how to evaluate themselves as well as group procedures.

Space is not available to illustrate by charts and diagrams, but help for making and using evaluation forms can be obtained from your denominational resources.

4. *Counseling, conversation, visitation.* Leaders, as well as members of the group, can learn a great deal from one another in conversations and visiting, and special problems may need counseling by the pastor or other competent person.

5. *Recreation and social activities.* How often adults are " discovered " when they participate in recreational and social activities of the group! Sometimes the discovery is painful; more often it reveals hidden resources. Adult groups have an obligation to provide activities that unleash many hidden interests and needs.

6. *Recognizing changing interests and needs.* Interests and needs of adults do not all " stay put." When a group can no longer minister to the changing interests and needs of several of its members, reorganization of some kind is essential. Young adults, for example, cease to be young adults by and by. The program that helped to meet their needs three or four years ago must be changed as they face up to new problems and potentialities.

## IMPLICATIONS OF THIS CHAPTER

1. *What adults need to know can become what they want to know.* When their interests and needs combine, the program for their spiritual maturing will enlist their co-operation.

2. *Adult interests are either assets or liabilities.* Christian education seeks to transform liabilities into assets by enlisting adults in accepting the disciplines of the Holy Spirit for their own growth in grace.

3. *Needs must be recognized as lacks.* To complete what is incomplete; to mature what is immature; to stimulate growth by supplying the spiritual vitamins essential for growth: these things adult education believes in doing

because these are processes through which the Holy Spirit can work.

4. *Needs may also reach the level of predicaments.* Entrenched evil in the world precipitates gigantic predicaments too complex for man to resolve by his best efforts. Faith gives him strength to persist, to die if need be, but to continue his trust in God.

5. *The gospel of Jesus Christ meets adult interests and needs, also man's predicaments.* Jesus' calm affirmation in John 16:33 has powerful comfort in it: " In the world you have tribulation; but be of good cheer, I have overcome the world."

CHAPTER
IV

## GOALS OF ADULT CHRISTIAN EDUCATION

*Goals help us to know and to see where we are headed;
only by setting goals can we hope to achieve success
in our church work.*

In preparing to write this text, correspondence was held
with a number of denominational directors of adult work.
One question they were asked was: *What goals in adult
education do you recommend to the local church?*

The responses clearly indicated that the eight general
objectives of Christian education approved by the International Council of Religious Education in 1930 had had
wide influence in determining the adult objectives of the
denominations. However, many of the denominations had
revised these to make them more usable by local churches
in their adult work. Many of the directors also stated that
they were "marking time" to await the adoption of the
revised objectives that will be forthcoming from the Division of Christian Education of the National Council of
Churches. A revision seemed necessary because of changes
that have taken place in the educational and theological
climate in which Christian education takes place. The nature of the church is being re-examined and described. Developmental psychology has uncovered new values in personality, and has suggested new processes to promote
spiritual growth. The mission of the church is being re-
studied. Christian education is now recognized as relevant
to the total task of the church. The relevance of the Holy

Spirit to successful group work is receiving greater emphasis.

For such reasons, and others not mentioned, it has become essential to restate and revise both the general objectives of Christian education and the age group objectives. Several years will elapse before this task is completed.

At the present time a fairly accurate picture can be drawn of what the denominations are recommending to the local churches. This will be done in this text by reporting what denominational directors are saying to their respective constituencies. The list is arranged in alphabetical order for convenience of reference. Any omission of denominations is due to lack of information at the time of writing. Also, the names of the denominations are as given before certain mergers, which are now in process, were effected.

By studying the statements that follow, the leaders of adults in local churches may be able to select goals that best meet local interests and needs, as well as those that serve denominational objectives.

### American Baptist

" We suggest about twelve goals in adult work each year, and challenge the local church committee on adult work to give consideration to the following items:

" Evaluation of the adult curriculum
  Study of adult rooms and equipment
  Reaching unreached adults
  Discovering competent teaching, class, and group leadership
  Leadership training and demonstration classes
  Organizing new classes and groups
  Planning for special family programs

" We send a yearly printed manual to local churches with the program spelled out, including a monthly schedule to follow."

*Church of God*
" Some of the primary needs of adults to which we need to give attention are:

" 1. Adults need to see the nature of the adulthood which they seek in our modern society and to know that the goal is impossible without the power of God in their lives.

" 2. Adults need to understand the pattern of their physical, mental, and social changes, the tasks which they are to achieve at the various levels of adulthood, and to find creative relationships within the context of the church.

" 3. Adults need to see the patterns of their personality development as individuals in their social setting and in the church.

" 4. Adults need to understand the meaning of Christian personality and what it means to be Christian.

" 5. Adults need to see the necessity for continuing to learn and grow and to understand the meaning of maturity, especially Christian maturity.

" 6. Adults need to be guided in their quest for meaning and in creative Christian growth in the church and in the world.

" In order to achieve these ends, some of the major goals in our work with adults in the local church are: ( *a* ) To confront them with the reality of God in Jesus Christ. The curriculum and the entire program for adults should aim at this. ( *b* ) To seek a response of faith and a definite commitment to Christ. ( *c* ) To aid adults in understanding themselves and their human situation, and to help them know that they fulfill life's highest purposes by living as

Christians. (*d*) To help them grow as sons of God. (*e*) To help adults live in the Spirit of God in every relationship, and to fulfill their common discipleship in the church and in the world. (*f*) To clarify constantly and make more meaningful the Christian hope in which Christians live and serve.

" When adults fully participate in the *life* and *work* of the church, then will these needs be met and these goals be realized in their lives; then will they bear effective Christian witness to the redemptive grace of God in daily Christian living and service."

### Church of the Nazarene

" For the first time in the history of our Department of Church Schools a director of adult work was appointed and began his work on February 15, 1955. Our Christian education objectives for adults, as outlined by Dr. A. F. Harper in *The Nazarene Sunday School,* are: (1) to know and love the Bible; (2) to help folks find God; (3) to encourage growth in grace; (4) to build members into the church; and (5) to reach new people."

### Congregational and Christian Churches

" Our basic view of Christian education is to enable persons to grow within the fellowship of the church. Our goals seek to produce: (*a*) enlightened churchmanship; (*b*) responsible citizenship; (*c*) meaningful fellowship; (*d*) rewarding recreation.

" Our local churches create such activities as: young adult, student organizations, couples clubs, mothers groups, family life program, parents classes, adult church school classes, discussion groups, hobby clubs, men's clubs, women's organizations, service groups, senior churchmen's classes, Golden-Age clubs, home department fellowships."

### Cumberland Presbyterian Church

" Our objectives in adult work are not yet specifically spelled out, but we seek to mediate them through our curriculum materials, and through direct relationship with local church adult directors. We emphasize: attention to grading and grouping; encouragement of the formation of adult study groups; a ministry to home members of the church; and the development of a program of Christian family life education."

### Disciples of Christ

" The goals we have followed for adults are the eight objectives of Christian education prepared by the International Council of Religious Education, and we are now working with the National Council of Churches in the revision of the objectives but have not worked out our own goals at the adult level as different from the ones that the National Council is preparing.

" In certain areas, however, we have specific goals related to adult activities:

"For the adult class: As a part of the church, the adult class shares in the chief purpose of the church, namely, to lead men to commit the whole of their lives to Christ so that they may live by his will. The adult class, therefore, must confront men with the whole gospel and lead them to appropriate the Word of God.

"For adult and family conferences/camps: The adult and family conferences/camps supplement the program of the local church, deepen the faith of indivduals, and broaden personal experiences in Christian living which lead to a fuller commitment to Christ and his way of life:

" By offering opportunities through personal enrichment and group activities for the individual to encounter new imperatives of the Christian faith by means of:

" self-examination,
rethinking his basic Christian beliefs,
facing up to the simple teachings of the Gospels.

" By offering intensified opportunities for Christian growth.

" By offering opportunities for the development of the lives of adults and family members as churchmen, resulting in a Christian community of fellowship.

" By offering opportunities for dynamic, creative experiences that will help persons become better leaders in the home, the church, the community, the nation, and the world."

## Evangelical and Reformed

" We shall be using the objectives for adult Christian education that are approved by the National Council of Churches, with such adaptations as may be needed in our administrative setup."

## Evangelical United Brethren

" To promote the achievement of adult goals, we recommend an adult director in each local church who chairs an adult council composed of persons who are the elected or recognized leaders of each adult group. This adult council seeks to unify the adult program which we call our Comprehensive Program for Adults."

## Friends

" Goals or objectives recommended to local meetings include growth to the measure of the stature of the fullness of Christ. In a Christian home each member is included in a togetherness, a little kingdom of love in which no one stands alone.

" We recommend to local leadership that they influence their members to be active Christians daily, to be ' tuned in ' on a spiritual wave length with the Master so that our lives reflect the messages of love and understanding that he communicates to each of us daily.

" Our active objectives include: (*a*) Adding books on Christian family life to the church library. (*b*) Each meeting (church) is encouraged to plan an annual Family Life Workshop. (*c*) Many couples clubs have been formed after these family workshops. These clubs give the desired church-influenced social contacts, keep the meeting abreast of new and good literature, and give a sort of group therapy to many. (*d*) We try to acquaint parents with the child's Sunday school activities and interests. (*e*) We try to interest parents in teaching religion in the home, in using family worship and daily devotions, and in becoming acquainted with good religious books, and with American Friends Service Committee packets, and such other helps as the Women's International League folder *Children's Books to Build for Peace*. Audio-visual aids on this subject are promoted also. (*f*) We encourage church leadership to prepare for counseling the membership."

*Methodist*

" The scope of our program for the Christian education of adults is based on the statement in our *Discipline:* ' The Division of the Local Church shall develop a comprehensive and unified program of Christian education which shall lead to a knowledge of the Holy Scriptures, the Christian religion, and the Christian church. It shall provide for worship, fellowship, study, and service, including social, recreational, evangelistic, and missionary activities and education in the Christian way of life. . . .'

" The general objectives should give guidance to leaders in local churches and enable them to develop specific objectives. The statement of objectives should serve this purpose.

" To help each person — child, youth, adult — to achieve an intimate acquaintanceship and fellowship with God as Heavenly Father, and fully to realize, in everyday life, the power of God's Spirit.

" To lead each person to accept Jesus Christ as his personal Savior, to acknowledge his supremacy, and to make a sincere effort to practice his teachings in all the relationships of life.

" To help parents and teachers to realize their opportunity and obligation to use every means possible, in the church and out of it, to cultivate right attitudes, to form right habits, to develop Christian character in growing life.

" To develop all our people in loyalty to the church, to build up the membership of the church, and to strengthen the church in all its undertakings.

" To create within our church members a passion to reach and bring into the local church every person within the range of its responsibility and to perfect ways and means of accomplishing this result.

" To develop within our people a sense of their obligation for civic and social righteousness, community service, and interracial friendship, and to provide programs through which these obligations may be discharged.

" To develop within our people a desire to share in the world-wide mission of the church, and to provide opportunities through which this desire may find satisfaction, to the end that the gospel may reach all mankind.

" To develop within our people a sense of comradeship between the local church and the church college, to the end that each in its place may effectively help the other in developing a people whose religious experience is grounded in a faith which is evangelical, reasonable, and unconquerable."

*Presbyterian Church in the United States*

" 1. To develop in persons an increasing knowledge, understanding, and love of the Bible as the inspired Word of God, the record of the way of salvation, and the guide for everyday living; and to lead them into an intelligent appreciation of extra-Biblical records of Christian experience.

" 2. To foster an understanding of a fellowship with God as Creator, Ruler, and Father, the supreme reality in daily experience, and the only true center of life.

" 3. To develop an appreciative understanding of the Person, teachings, life, death, and resurrection of Jesus Christ the Son of God, so as to result in acceptance of him as Savior from sin and the Lord of life, and in conduct that shows love and loyalty to him and his cause.

" 4. To foster in persons a realization of the presence of the Holy Spirit, and of his power to regenerate men dead in sin, and to bring about a progressive and continuous development of character in harmony with the teachings and example of Jesus, as set forth in the Scriptures, resulting in a continued effort to be Christlike in all the relationships of life.

" 5. To develop in persons an ability and willingness to incorporate into everyday living the fact of God's fatherly concern for all men and the Scriptural teaching concerning man's obligation as a Christian to his fellow man, so for every individual and the church there shall be stressed the development of Christian attitudes in all social relationships, including domestic, racial, economic, political, and international.

" 6. To develop in persons an ability and disposition to participate in the organized society of Christian believers

— the church — as the fellowship without which adequate Christian nurture cannot take place.

" 7. To develop in persons a recognition and acceptance of the evangelistic and missionary responsibility of each Christian and the church, in accordance with the Great Commission and the nature of the Christian gospel.

" 8. To develop in persons a Christian interpretation of life, man, and the universe, an acceptance of God's purposes and plans for life, and a conscious effort to carry out these plans.

" 9. To develop in growing persons an appreciation of the meaning and importance of the Christian family, and the ability and disposition to participate in and contribute constructively to the life of this primary group."

### Presbyterian Church in the U.S.A.

" The goal of Christian adult education is to lead persons to a personal commitment to Jesus Christ as their Lord and Savior. Such commitment involves a continuing growth in the understanding and acceptance of the obligations and opportunities of Christian discipleship, as well as understanding of, and participation in, the beloved community, the church.

" Specifically applied to the adult program of the local church, this means that such a program must be relevant at two points: (1) It must be relevant to the Word which the church exists to proclaim. (2) It must be relevant to the recognized and unrecognized needs of adults.

" Too often we tend to stress one of them to the exclusion of the other, so that much that happens in some adult groups ignores the existential realities of the lives persons live, while in other groups the unique word of the gospel is lost under a pretense of Christian fellowship or activity.

" Perhaps the most serious practical concern with which

we must deal, if adults are to be led to reflective commitment, is the tendency to atomize the adult by the plethora
of activities in our often overorganized churches."

*Protestant Episcopal Church*

" Three basic objectives of a parish program for adult
education aim:

" 1. To provide opportunities for enabling the adult to
become a ' new man ' through confrontation with the
gospel.

" 2. To assist the adult through participation in learning
situations and activities to have an increasing understanding and concern for the nature and heritage of the Christian church.

" 3. To respond to and participate in the ' Community
of God's People ' in fulfilling the mission of the church to
all men."

*Reformed Church in America*

" We advise each local church to survey the job that
needs to be done with adults, and then formulate their
own objectives in the light of specific needs."

*United Church of Canada*

" The goal in adult education recommended to the local
church is the general goal that is included in the constitu-
tion of the Board of Christian Education — ' That every individual, at each stage of his developing life, may be led
to know and love and serve God as revealed in Jesus
Christ.'

" The only particular description of goal is that which
the Young Adult Committee has expressed for couples club
and young adult fellowships as follows:

" The purpose of the young adult fellowship in the

church is to relate young adults to God as revealed in Jesus Christ, to one another, and to the life and work of the church.

" This fellowship provides an organization through which young adults may be integrated into the church's total life and make their distinctive contribution by giving leadership to Christian living and action in the home, the church, and the community.

" The young adult program which accomplishes these objectives will include: Christian fellowship, Christian thought, Christian action."

### United Lutheran Church in America

" There is in existence no official statement of goals for recommendation to local congregations, but we have generally presented these:

" 1. *To guide adults into Christian faith and life.* This includes: an understanding of the Bible, the Christian faith, and a Christian view of life; loyalty to Christ, the church, and Christian ideals; citizenship; problem solution; skills for living and serving; Christian attitudes and appreciations; ability to work with people; use of leisure time.

" 2. *To bring about a Christian society and world.* This includes: recognition of the Fatherhood of God and the brotherhood of man; appreciation of Christian altruism; democratic ideals based on the worth and needs of people; readiness to settle differences on the basis of Christian principles and negotiation; a peaceful world.

" 3. *To make family life Christian and efficient.* This includes: guidance in Christian marriage and family life; cooperation between church and home; home guidance of children and youth; a whole linkage with the community."

### United Presbyterian Church of North America

"We make use of the general objectives of Christian education that have been adopted interdenominationally, and adapt these to our adult program."

### National Council of Churches

Through the Division of Christian Education of the National Council of Churches adult work has a portfolio. The main function is to be a co-ordinating agency through which denominational directors of adult work may find a common meeting ground for clearance, planning, and mutual assistance.

### How to State Goals in Local Churches

The line of least resistance, obviously, is to accept the statement of goals suggested in your denominational materials for the local church. Your denominational headquarters would prefer, however, that you rework, restate, and adapt anything they suggest so that the final list of goals or objectives is really yours.

The preferred way of selecting objectives for adult work in the local church is to place the responsibility in the council on adult work so that every area of adult work will be included. The statement of goals for adult Christian education as a whole may be in general terms. The spelling out will be done by each organization that enlists adults in its program.

To illustrate, one goal might be stated, *to enlist all adults in our congregation in some form of Bible study.* To accomplish this general goal several organizations would offer Bible study, and additional provision would be made for Bible study outside the regular schedule — special courses during Lent, or in the fall, spring, or winter school of religion.

Another goal, as stated by the council on adult work,

might be, *to challenge our homes to accept more responsibility for the Christian nurture of the members of the family*. Obviously, a number of the organizations are working with families. To achieve this goal co-operative effort will be needed among church school leaders, the pastor, the church officers, men's work, women's work, young adults, middle-aged adults, and so on.

Thus the list of goals will grow into a grass-roots statement of adult objectives for the local church. The local list should be checked and compared with denominational and interdenominational lists so that the product will represent the best thinking of all who are working with adults.

## WHAT THIS CHAPTER MEANS

1. *The local church is the place where adult Christian education is most likely to be generated, but its field of operation is wherever adults live, work, play, and worship.* Adult education has more chance of happening if local church leaders of adults are diligent to study the interests and needs of adults, and then list the goals or objectives that they will try to achieve over a period of years.

2. *Denominational directors of adult work serve local churches.* Their most valuable contribution is to challenge local churches to develop programs that meet adult interests and needs. Through printed materials, conferences, schools, correspondence, and otherwise, the local church leaders of adults are kept informed and inspired. But no denominational director can do for a local church what it must learn to do for itself.

3. *Denominations are learning from one another.* Denominational adult work directors get together frequently in interdenominational gatherings. They exchange experiences and stimulate one another. Each denomination has

a stronger program of adult work because of these co-operative conferences. Local churches in a community may also learn from one another. All who are working with adults in a local community should meet together occasionally to have their horizons lifted.

4. *Co-operation with one's denominational program is best in the long run.* This means at least: being on the mailing list; attending conferences and leadership schools; reporting significant happenings; and so on. And it also means that your local church will be left free to expand its adult program beyond denominational boundaries if interests and needs warrant. In such manner local churches help make the history of adult Christian education.

## THE COUNCIL ON ADULT WORK

All the varieties of adult work must be correlated in the
local church; it is the laboratory for adult education.

Denominational and interdenominational programs of
adult work largely determine what local churches will un-
dertake with their adults. Obviously the national programs
have not been created in an ivory tower; they have been
hammered out on the anvil of countless conferences with
local representatives. This is as it should be, as it must be.
But the time finally arrives when the consensus of delibera-
tions must jell, and a manual of adult work, or a reasonable
facsimile of such, must go to the printer. Then follows an
anxious period of promoting the use of the manual in local
churches. Leaders and potential leaders in local churches
are assembled, together with their subdistrict, district,
conference, presbytery, synod, and field men and women,
and others. They discuss the best ways to make the local
program tick.

Responsibility for the Christian education of adults generally has to be shouldered by directors of adult work in
the denomination. Furthermore, directors of adult work
are on the staffs of boards of Christian education, by and
large. This necessitates that boards of Christian education
spark the conferences that bring representatives of different agencies together to explain the whys and wherefores
of a local church adult program. But these representatives

may also be involved in local church men's work, women's work, missionary education, and social education and action. Seldom are these interests the direct responsibility of adult work as such.

As a consequence, adult leaders in local churches raise questions like these:

" How is men's work related to this local church adult program? We have a going men's organization."

" How is women's work involved? Our women's organization has its own program of study, missions, action, and service."

" Who is to promote stewardship education, which we consider to be in our local church the foundation not only of our budget-raising, but also of enlisting people in giving their time and abilities? "

" Is missionary education also adult education, or is this a specialized field that has to be promoted separately? "

" Our young adult groups, couples clubs, hobby groups, bowling teams, and so forth, are fellowship groups more or less connected to the church. Are they to be incorporated locally in adult work? "

" Adult classes have their own membership; select their own study courses; promote parties. Are they to come under the umbrella of adult work in the local church? "

" Would it be better to confine adult work to study groups, and concentrate our efforts in the local church on making them educationally efficient? "

" The congregation that meets regularly for corporate worship: obviously this is the pastor's responsibility in counsel with one or more of the official boards of the church. The majority of the congregation are adults. Many of them are not members of any of the organizations. Does local adult work have a concern for corporate worship? "

" Then there are the official boards: they are mostly

adult. They have important functions to perform, and need to be trained to discharge their duties. Who will train them? Is local adult work responsible? "

" The teachers in the church school; the leaders of youth organizations; leaders of men's and women's organizations: how will they receive their training? Has local adult work a stake in this training? "

These and many other questions of similar import are not academic. They arise constantly in all the denominations. What is the answer?

## The Denominational Answer

Each denomination answers these questions according to its administrative framework. No two denominations answer exactly alike. This does not imply that one denomination has better answers than another; it says simply that each denomination gives the best answers it can to its local churches. Furthermore, the denominational directors of adult work are keeping their plans and thinking in a fluid state, so that, in time, some of the questions that have persisted in local churches will be answered.

## Co-ordinating the Adult Program in the Local Church

Without exception, we believe, denominations are recommending that their local churches co-ordinate their adult work. This requires a *council* or *committee* that represents all the adults in the local church. It should be administratively related to the governing body of the local church, and presumably to the committee on Christian education. The chairman of the adult committee or council should be a member of the committee on Christian education, where denominational patterns of organization authorize such procedure.

Committees on Christian education in local churches are numerous, but councils or committees on adult work seem to be less common. In many churches with several adult study classes there may be an adult department, but the officers of this department do not necessarily function as a committee on adult work. They confine themselves to the business of promoting adult classes. No indictment is lodged against them on this score; we do hesitate to encourage them to think that they are *the* committee or council on adult work.

Since denominations are so universally recommending a local church committee or council on adult work, how is such a committee to be composed, and what are its main functions?

### The Committee or Council on Adult Work

In general, allowing for denominational patterns, the committee on adult work will include:

A *chairman:* He or she will usually be a member of the committee on Christian education. He should not be selected to represent any particular phase of adult work, but be a person who is willing to prepare himself, or has prepared himself, for administering all the facets of adult work that it is desirable to include in the committee's outreach.

A *representative of adult church school classes:* He or she may be an officer in one of the classes, or just a member of one. Preferably, perhaps, he should be the superintendent of the adult department, or one of its officers.

A *young adult representative:* With young adult fellowships, couples clubs, younger parents groups now in so many local churches, this member of the committee would represent the entire young adult constituency.

An *older adult:* Even though the local church may have no organized work among older adults as such, the time has surely arrived for them to be represented in a committee on adult work. They have needs and interests that can easily be neglected unless they are in the thinking and planning of the adult program.

*A representative of men's work:* All men are adults. Although the program of men's work has administrative lines connecting it with denominational men's work, in the local church these lines are less visible, and adult education as such has something to contribute to men's organizations.

*A representative of women's work:* What was stated about men's work has the same connotations for women's work to be represented on the committee on adult work. Because women in their organized work are using methods and materials of adult education, they have much to contribute to a committee on adult work.

*The pastor, director of religious education, or other staff member:* Whether ex officio or official, a representative of the pastor's office naturally belongs on the committee. The worshiping congregation is a fertile field for adult education that trains in worship, evangelism, fellowship, and especially in learning how to use divinely given means of grace.

Already seven members have been nominated for this committee. In smaller churches the number can be decreased; in larger churches it may need to be increased.

Some denominations would recommend for membership a representative: of the home department; or the middle-aged adults; or social education and action; or missionary education; or family life; or stewardship; or evangelism. A few might think it was a good idea to have a youth representative on the adult committee, for obvious reasons.

*What Will the Adult Committee or Council Do?*

Before it begins to make recommendations, or upset apple carts, the committee needs to get acquainted with itself. If the idea of fellowship, *koinōnia,* is valid for all adult work, it should begin and continue in the committee. No member, regardless of what he represents, is there to get something for his constituency at the expense of others. Neither are members to try to trade privileges. The chairman can contribute something great by helping to mold the members into a *koinōnia.* But this kind comes not without the work of the Holy Spirit.

*The meetings of the committee* should be conducted by using approved procedures of education. Every method available should be explored and tested. Perchance, if a method will not work in the committee on adult work, it might not work in other adult groups. Therefore the adult committee will be a practicing laboratory of adult education.

*Its first major activity* is to learn what the adult organizations of the church, including the church school, are doing. Representatives of these on the committee will prepare chart diagrams describing: number and sex of adults enrolled; scope of the program; schedule of meetings; leadership, actual and needed; curriculum used, or program materials available; methods of conducting meetings of organization; potential of unreached; budget; service and recreational activities; and any other pertinent facts.

This activity will also serve to create the *koinōnia* within the adult committee. As each describes what is happening, much of which will surely be commendable, and some things not so promising, the committee will begin to dream dreams and see visions. Then they will be reminded of the ancient prophecy of Joel that Peter quoted on the Day of Pentecost:

" ' and your young men shall see visions,
  and your old men shall dream dreams;
  yea, and on my menservants and my maidservants
        in those days
  I will pour out my Spirit; and they shall prophesy.' "

It may take three or four meetings of the committtee to gather and digest information about the work of the organizations, but it will be time well invested. The purpose is to establish an adult committee that, with changing members over the years, will function as long as the local church exists. No cutting of corners must be tolerated. All chairmen please take notice!

*Having discovered and visualized organizational programs,* the committee may then proceed to chart their future course. Activities may include:

1. Securing the names, addresses, vocations, avocations, and other data of every adult in the church constituency. Preferably the names should be listed on 4" × 6" cards which can be filed. The organizations can submit their respective enrollments, which will lighten the task. Through the church roll the remainder of the names can be located.

2. Distributing to each adult an interest finder. The committee can make one, or use can be made of a standard form, usually available from denominational headquarters or from interdenominational resources. Distribution should be authorized by the pastor and official boards. Set a time schedule for returns, and be prepared for mopping up, human nature being what it is.

3. When the interest finders are returned, then begins the arduous task of collating, transferring data to the name cards, and analyzing what is discovered. The members of the committee may enlist many others to help them in this

collation. High school students can quickly learn the techniques.

4. When the data are all assembled, and the committee has met again, a large chalkboard, or preferably large sheets of paper, should be available to visualize the findings. The crosshatch illustration, "Program Planning Chart," opposite, is a sample of how to visualize data. The perpendicular column will list the interests and needs as given by those who returned the interest finders. The committee may decide that there are omissions; if so, additional interests and needs should be listed with crayon of a different color. The horizontal column pictures the organizations, the pastor and staff, that are carrying, or should carry, the main responsibility for ministering to the interests and needs.

With such a picture staring the committee in the face, ideas and plans will begin to germinate for developing the larger program of adult work.

5. A strategy is next in order for approaching the organizations to lay before their leaders all that the data reveal that is of primary concern to them. Can this particular organization accept its share of improving the program for its adults? Obviously, there would be no sense in trying to create a new organization if an existing one can do the job. No doubt the pastor will have discovered many ways in which he can adapt his program to fit more efficiently into the adult work program.

6. When sufficient time has elapsed to give the existing organizations their opportunity, then the committee may find necessity for proposing additional organizations or activities, both of a formal and informal nature. In such manner, over a lapse of months, and even years, the adult work program unfolds.

7. While the committee is inching its way through this

## PROGRAM PLANNING CHART

| ADULT INTERESTS AND NEEDS | Pastor | Bible Study Groups | Other Study Groups | Young Adult Fellowship | Men's Organization | Women's Organization | Older Adult Clubs | Family Nights | Lenten Meetings | Communicants Classes | Official Boards | Meetings in Homes | Leadership Classes | Social Action Groups |
|---|---|---|---|---|---|---|---|---|---|---|---|---|---|---|
| Understanding Basic Theology | X | X | | | | | X | X | | | | | | |
| Knowledge and Use of the Bible | X | X | | X | | | X | X | | X | | | | |
| Private and Public Prayer | | | | | | | | | | | | | | |
| Utilizing the Means of Grace | | | | | | | | | | | | | | |
| Church History | | | | | | | | | | | | | | |
| Private and Corporate Worship | | | | | | | | | | | | | | |
| Stewardship | | | | | | | | | | | | | | |
| Church Officer Training | | | | | | | | | | | | | | |
| Vocational Guidance | | | | | | | | | | | | | | |
| Friendship and Fellowship | | | | | | | | | | | | | | |
| Rewarding Recreation | | | | | | | | | | | | | | |
| Ecumenical Movement | | | | | | | | | | | | | | |
| Christian Citizenship | | | | | | | | | | | | | | |
| Speaking in Public | | | | | | | | | | | | | | |
| Leading a Group | | | | | | | | | | | | | | |
| Church Membership | | | | | | | | | | | | | | |
| Hobbies | | | | | | | | | | | | | | |
| Vocal and Instrumental Music | | | | | | | | | | | | | | |
| Other Denominations | | | | | | | | | | | | | | |
| World Religions | | | | | | | | | | | | | | |
| Missionary Education | | | | | | | | | | | | | | |
| Social Education | | | | | | | | | | | | | | |
| Parental Guidance | | | | | | | | | | | | | | |
| Family Problems | | | | | | | | | | | | | | |
| Minority Groups | | | | | | | | | | | | | | |
| National and International Relations | | | | | | | | | | | | | | |

RESPONSIBILITY

maze of problems, there are a few leading questions it must not avoid:

a. Will our church be able to enlist more or fewer adults in the next decade because of community population trends?

b. What will be our attitude toward enlisting people who have not previously been " our kind "?

c. What will be our building and equipment needs, and what budget is necessary?

d. How can we enlist and train the leaders?

Local situations will generate other questions. Your denominational resources must be constantly consulted. Some of the denominations have already prepared excellent manuals or pamphlets for their local church adult committees. Get them; use them.

It will take patience, courage, foresight, and faith to launch out into the deep of adult work. If the committee dies a-borning, it will be one more casualty on the high seas of adult work, but it will have cast away a precious opportunity to minister to the church's largest constituency. These casualties need not occur if the committee is prepared to work in sweat, blood, and tears.

> " The heights by great men reached and kept
> Were not attained by sudden flight,
> But they, while their companions slept,
> Were toiling upward in the night."
> — *Longfellow*

Many night meetings will be the fate of any group that plans and promotes a comprehensive, local church program for adults.

### Beyond Organizations

If any leader of adults concludes from reading this chapter that organizations are the total answer for effective adult work in the local church, we hasten to lift a warning finger. Theoretically, a local church might succeed in enlisting every adult in one or more organizations and still be far from the goals of the Christian education of adults. Success depends on purposeful enlistment, educational guidance, and the disciplines of the Holy Spirit, not on simply " joining up." To involve adults uncritically in activities violates the integrity of the adult, and compromises the purpose of the church and the gospel that the church exists to proclaim. We already have too much worship of organizations and not enough concern for the church as the church. An excuse is often made that by enlisting adults in organizations they will become interested in the church. Too often we have seen the logic backfire. Would it not be better to lift up the church in the estimation of adults, and then the organizations would serve the larger purpose of the church?

*Postscript*

Lest we forget something of supreme importance, we are reminding the adult committee that it is not an independent entity. It is actually a subcommittee (emphasis on *sub*) of the committee on Christian education. Every plan of the adult committee should be submitted to the parent group. Reports should be made regularly. The necessity for these matters need not be labored. The committee on Christian education carries responsibility for the total program of education of children, youth, and adults. The different subcommittees must plan and work in harmony.

## IMPLICATIONS FOR THE LOCAL CHURCH

1. *Planning a comprehensive program of adult education requires locating the adults, knowing their interests*

*and needs, and enlisting them.* There will be much surveying, circulating of questionnaires, visitation, making of card indexes, and keeping of records.

2. *Developing an effective program means years of sustained effort.* Co-operation of all existing organizations, as well as new ones, will be needed. Building and equipment must be projected, and leaders obtained and trained for their respective responsibilities.

3. *Continuing evaluation of an adult program is essential to success.* If adult education is what we claim it to be, then those participating in the program will be growing persons. The interests and needs of yesterday will become the achievements of tomorrow. The program must be kept fluid so that it can flow into new channels as new needs arise.

## GROUPING ADULTS

"For where two or three are gathered in my name,
there am I in the midst of them." — *Matt. 18:20.*

The purpose of this chapter is to explore how a local
church can group its adults for more effective adult education.

Sociologists have been telling us for decades that the
group is the essential environment for human development. They speak of *primary,* or face-to-face groups; *sec-
ondary,* where relationships are not so intimate; *peer*
groups, in which the members are theoretically equals;
and so on. The family is a primary group and exerts more
influence for good or ill on its members than any other
group. Schools and churches are usually classified as sec-
ondary, but highly important. Within schools and churches
are many peer groups, molding those who participate.

Churches do not provide, nor should they, all the groups
to which their members may belong. Community and vocational responsibilities require numerous groupings in
which Christian men and women associate with their
peers of all faiths and no faiths. In such groups Christian
vocation has opportunity to witness to the gospel that is
professed.

Church leaders are studying the findings of sociology,
psychology, philosophy, and other disciplines to supplement their use of theology. They recognize that every discovery that throws light on the nature of man is relevant
to the use of God's revelation to help man become what

God has purposed for him. In essence a program of Christian education is utilization of methods and materials to implement the gospel as it has come to us through the revelation of God in Christ. For its methods it will draw upon every resource that educators in any field have discovered and used successfully. The future will open more avenues of help. As long as Christian education holds to its Christian objectives, it can use methods that have been developed in other disciplines without mental reservations.

## Why Is Grouping Needed?

A group must be more than a collection of individuals who have been assembled by various inducements and enticements, and whose motives for joining the group are "mixed," to say the least. Perhaps many adult groups have to begin by inducing people to join who would never take the step on their own initiative. A large number of people join a group because they do not have enough "sales resistance" to refuse the invitation of a friend.

Obviously this method of organizing a group has some disadvantages, but it cannot be avoided completely. We must help adults overcome their lethargy and indifference.

The primary purpose of forming adult groups is to attain an objective that could not be achieved by individual efforts. In one of the denominations the objective of group work with adults was classified into four parts: (1) enlightened churchmanship; (2) responsible citizenship; (3) meaningful fellowship; (4) rewarding recreation. Under this umbrella can be gathered about everything that churches are obligated to attempt with adults and for them. Whether they are young, middle aged, or older, they have needs that these four objectives encompass. The value of such a classification is the help it offers, both to denominational directors and to local churches, in visualiz-

ing to everybody the direction for adult education to proceed.

## A Look at Our Traditional Adult Groupings

The adult groupings that Protestant churches have developed through many decades are the result of growing
needs of men and women, and of growing demands upon
the church to enlarge its ministry and its outreach. It was
not until 1780 that Sunday schools were thought of. Adult
Bible classes were a much later development. Men's work
and women's work are a comparatively new phenomenon
in church life and work. And the church's concern in the
use of leisure time had to run the gantlet of the entrenched
conviction of church leaders that "play was the devil's
opportunity to tempt good people to do wrong."

Now that we have several traditional adult groupings in
all our local churches, we are compelled in honesty to the
church's mission and ministry to inquire whether they
need re-evaluation and, probably, transformation or even
liquidation in some cases. The Ladies' Aid, to cite one example, formerly was the major "women's work" in most
Protestant churches. The nomenclature is rapidly becoming obsolete, not because women have ceased to enlist in
the necessary activities that a Ladies' Aid performed, but
because an enlarging mission required a woman's organization with more scope. Dare we also say that traditional
adult Bible classes, once serving a necessary purpose in
the form in which they exist, must now rethink and re-
evaluate their program? There are needs of adults that
cannot be fully met in a traditional Bible class. Either the
class must enlarge its program, and make its organization more flexible, or it must concede the right of some
adults with special needs to group themselves into other
patterns.

The growing practice of short-term interest and study groups is evidence that the traditional groupings of adults are yielding to the claims of interests and needs.

Bible study will be a must as long as time lasts. How adults can best be grouped for Bible study is the primary question every local church must face. Men's work, women's work, programs for young adults, middle-aged and older adults, will certainly remain an integral part of Christian education indefinitely. How to keep these groupings from becoming "institutionalized" is the business of adults who comprise them.

When men and women attend an organization to "keep it going," something serious is wrong with the organization. Its objective should be to "keep them going."

### Which Are "Priority" Groups for Adults?

This *is* a question. Corporate worship is essential for the spiritual maturing of adults; therefore every adult who is able to attend should be in his place regularly. Although the congregation assembled for worship is not an adult organization as such, it may be classified as a grouping essential to adult growth, and an important element in adult education. Apparently many adults agree to this in principle but violate it in practice. They do so at their peril, because corporate worship is an appointment with God that no one can keep by proxy.

The next priority includes group Bible study, prayer, and consequent fellowship. A survey of denominational leaders indicates that in some communions a high proportion of adults are enlisted in Bible study; in others not more than ten per cent can be accounted for. Encouraging is the serious attention being given in all denominations to provide better Bible-study helps, improved methods, trained leadership, and more opportunities for elective

Bible courses. Bible study is also provided in many adult groups that are not Bible classes as such. In these groups it is recognized that its objectives can be achieved only as the members are in speaking communication with the Holy Spirit, who makes the Bible come alive in the situations where men and women live.

Beyond these two priorities Protestant churches permit a great deal of freedom of choice to adults, allowing them to determine the other groups that are essential to meet special needs and interests.

## How Many Adult Groups in a Local Church?

The denomination to which a local church belongs determines to a large extent the kind of adult groups, and the number. The size of the local church is another determinant, also the ages and needs of the adult constituency. Many suburban churches of recent origin, or new churches in industrial communities, may have a large proportion of young parents and few older people. Long-established churches usually have many older adults as well as young and middle-aged people.

The denominational director does not pretend to hand down a pattern that must be rigidly followed in local churches. Rather, the churches are encouraged specifically to develop their own program for adults.

When we view the scene from the perspective of an interdenominational survey of adult groupings in local churches, we are amazed at what has been happening in the last two or three decades. And the end is not yet. The most phenomenal growth has been among young adults and families. Even single young adults, men and women in the Armed Services, and employed women's groups are frequently mentioned.

Organizations for older people are growing rapidly, including summer camps and conferences.

Church officers are being indoctrinated in the nature, order, and nurture of the church, so that they may know the Biblical foundations on which to discharge their administrative responsibilities as participants in the church's ministry.

Adult groups, trained to visit in homes, are strengthening the evangelistic outreach of the church in the community. This is a lay movement in the best traditions of the " apostolic succession."

Choirs and other musical organizations enlist large numbers of adults.

Schools of religion, universities of life, and similar educational opportunities, offered for a week of consecutive meetings, or strung over a period of weeks, appeal especially to adult groups which are not really " organized " but are fellowships of study in Bible, missions, world religions, current problems, and so on.

Practically all the teachers in the church school are adults. They have their organizations for leadership training and conference.

Retreats of many kinds, some to plan for the future work of the church, some for spiritual enrichment and fellowship, are another form of adult grouping.

Some churches report regular luncheon clubs for men or women, held at a downtown restaurant on a week day or night.

Communicants classes, sometimes extending for ten or more sessions, help to prepare adults who are coming into the church membership. This is a splendid way of indoctrinating members in church history, polity, and membership privileges and responsibilities.

Men's work is being rethought in all denominations. In place of the traditional roast beef dinner, cooked and served by the women, followed by a popular address on most any subject that would draw a crowd, men are being organized in churchmanship. They are being taught to undergird the total church program with their service, giving, and intelligent participation. Men still need church dinners; such will be provided. But the Kingdom of Heaven is quite a bit more than eating and drinking.

Women's work is probably the most efficiently organized and administered of all adult groupings. It includes a balanced program to meet women's interests and needs in churchmanship, missions, social service, and community welfare. Their leaders go to school; they produce high-caliber materials; and they enlist a large proportion of the women.

For the purposes of this discussion it is unnecessary to continue listing adult groupings that local churches have developed. We asked at the beginning of this section, " How many adult groups in a local church? " Our object was to stimulate thinking. It would seem that the number of adult groups will be determined by exploring such questions as these:

1. How many adult groups are essential to supply the varied interests and needs of our adult constituency?

2. What adult groups are necessary to discharge our responsibility as a church to the community?

3. To further the work of our denomination, what adult groups must we have?

4. To be a co-operative denomination in the ecumenical movement, what adult groupings must we consider?

Such questions, and others that can be raised, attempt to take the long-range view of adult work. Whatever we have that is working well, we shall keep for the present. Whatever adult organization is slipping, or has outworn its usefulness, we shall reorganize or liquidate. This may sound ruthless and heartless, but certainly not more so than the words of Jesus on one occasion: "I am the vine, you are the branches. He who abides in me, and I in him, he it is that bears much fruit, for apart from me you can do nothing. . . . Every branch of mine that bears no fruit, he takes away, and every branch that does bear fruit he prunes, that it may bear more fruit." — John 15:5, 2.

Some adult organizations that have ceased to bear fruit can be honorably discharged. Those that give promise of bearing fruit, if pruned, can become useful again. New organizations must be planted as the ministries of the church require.

### How Much " Belonging " Is Wise?

To prevent a willing adult from being " fragmentized," some limit must be placed on the number of adult groupings to which he should belong. The competent man or woman, the born leader, the generous-hearted soul, is likely to be wanted in more adult groupings than he has time or energy to attend and participate. At the other extreme is the adult who " crashes " every meeting, invitation or no invitation.

How much belonging does an adult need for his own spiritual maturing? The two priorities — corporate worship and Bible study, prayer and fellowship — are essentials. Beyond these the man or woman must face up to the responsibilities for additional means for supplying his needs, and for carrying his share of the church's load. The church school needs teachers; the church must have trained officers; men's work and women's work are scarcely electives for all. Denominational and interdenominational agencies require many lay people to serve on their boards and committees. Church men and women are always in demand to participate in community agencies.

The decision to belong to an adult group in a local church must rest with the lay man or woman. Pressuring them to join is unethical, and it violates the right of individual conscience. On the other hand, two things at least can be done. First, the adult can be informed of the need the organization has for gifts such as he possesses; secondly, the committee or council on adult work can prepare a list of adults from which organizations can seek to "draft" members. In many churches there are unused talents of men and women — unused because nobody knows about them, or nobody brings them to the attention of organizations that could readily use them.

The potential of men and women in churches is commensurate with the churches' needs, when and if this potential is discovered and utilized. Russell H. Conwell's *Acres of Diamonds* still has a message for adult work in local churches.

In Chapter V, "The Council on Adult Work," it was suggested that the committee secure a complete card index of all the adults. On such a card would appear some of the potentialities that would not otherwise come to light.

If this discussion is encouraging some men and women to "resign" from certain adult groups, let it not be to get out of work, but to do more competent work for the Lord in more concentrated form. We hope, however, that many men and women who are shirking their organizational opportunities will be challenged to join up and go to work.

### Methods of Group Work

Methods are ways of enlisting men and women to achieve the spiritual maturing that God has provided for them through the school of the church. No method is sacrosanct in itself. Even preaching, which is divinely ordained, is not a set method. There are varieties of ways to preach.

Some are obviously better than others.

Methods are tools to accomplish objectives. Some tools are for one purpose, others for quite different uses. To use a tool for sawing a board that was intended to drive nails through the board is plain ignorance. It is also pretty disastrous to the board. Group leaders and members will be wise to possess a variety of methods, because there are many kinds of adults, and objectives have to be stated in harmony with the needs to be satisfied.

The purpose of this book does not include detailed discussion of methods because that is the province of other books in the series. Enough must be said, however, to indicate the relationship of methods to successful group work.

### Traditional Methods in Group Work

The church has had a not-too-magnificent obsession that knowledge could be imparted, and that correct knowledge would result in righteous conduct. For a century or so after the origin of the Sunday school in 1780, the prevailing method of teaching was to " tell " people what was good for them to know. Accompanying this method was the belief that Scripture stored in the memory would be recalled when needed to meet life's problems. There must have been some virtue in this method because our forebears in large numbers turned out pretty well. (Unrepentant dissenters maintain that they turned out well in spite of the methods, not because of them.)

The lecture method has had to stand a lot of criticism from educators because it seems to follow the tradition that the impartation of knowledge is the chief end of teaching. Now that we think we have discovered how people learn, we do not discard the lecture method as of no value, but use it for the purpose for which this tool was designed — primarily to provide information when it is needed to satisfy factual needs. When the lecture is interesting; when the lecturer is competent; when the group is inspired — the lecture or address may be just the method to get results. But if the lecturer proceeds to try to " moralize " adults into action, he has ignorantly gone too far with his tool. Adults must be given their opportunity to decide what is best to do with the information they have learned. This will demand tools such as discussion, workshops, further reading, surveys, field trips, hearings, forums, panels, role-playing, and whatever else can be profitably used.

Something should also be said about traditional patterns of organization. In the past it was presumed that every organization had to have a chairman or president, a vice-president, secretary, treasurer, and a number of committees. This is still necessary in some adult groups, but by no means in all of them. Every existing adult group should re-evaluate its pattern of organization to determine whether it furthers the needs of the group as a *koinōnia*, or if new patterns might improve group efficiency.

## The Growing Edge of Group Work

Where Christian education is taking hold of adult groups, new patterns of organization and procedure are being tried and tested. In some forward-moving churches, adult groupings are constantly changing membership. The curriculum is projected to meet adult interests and needs as they are discovered, and adults with similar needs meet for a month, three months, a year, to study and learn together. Then new groupings are formed to satisfy expanding needs and interests.

This plan may seem to " wreck " organized work because it does not demand sustained membership in the same group over a period of years. There are few "anniversaries" to celebrate, and no fifty-year "history" to publish. The redeeming value of the method is its enlistment of a large proportion of adults in their own planned education. They come to think of themselves as the *church* at study and work, even though a particular group may have no more than eight or twelve in number. Their loyalty is to the church first, because they are a part of it and not a fringe organization.

This plan does not "wreck" men's work, women's work, and other umbrella organizations. Neither does it displace established Bible-study classes that serve the needs of those who find more satisfaction in this type of group work. It serves as the growing edge of a movement that may expand into new horizons of adult education. And it also goes far toward solving the problem of "grading" adults.

### Group Leadership

Some wag once described a university as Mark Hopkins on one end of a log and a student on another. This was intended as a tribute to leadership.

Groups need leaders, but they do not necessarily prosper with the same leader for an extended time; and they get nowhere if the leader dominates them. One of the excellent values that has emerged from the ongoing experimentation in group procedures is the role of the leader. First of all, he is a member of the group. Secondly, he studies each member of his group, and assists them to know and respect one another; he helps each member to know and evaluate himself. In the group meeting the leader suggests but does not decide. He accepts criticism of himself, and permits criticism among group members according to democratic principles. He encourages cross-fire questions and discussion. When questions arise that cannot be immediately answered, he shows no embarrassment, but is glad to guide the group into research to discover the answers. He helps the group to arrive at some working conclusions; but the conclusions are theirs and his, not his alone, not theirs alone.

In succeeding chapters much more will be said about leadership as the discussion moves into the areas of beginning adulthood, continuing adulthood, and older adulthood.

## A New Testament Description of a Group

A profound picture of a Christian group is painted for us in Eph. 2:19–22: " So then you are no longer strangers and sojourners, but you are fellow citizens with the saints and members of the household of God, built upon the foundation of the apostles and prophets, Christ Jesus himself being the chief cornerstone, in whom the whole structure is joined together and grows into a holy temple in the Lord; in whom you also are built into it for a dwelling place of God in the Spirit."

We Christians must never rest content to group adults without keeping before us the main objective of our work — to build them "for a dwelling place of God in the Spirit."

This is a tested theology for grouping adults.

### IMPLICATIONS

1. *Grouping adults is essential to their Christian education and spiritual maturing.* Outside the fellowship there is no " salvation." This does not imply that every man must enroll in the men's organization, or every woman in the women's society, although more of each could do it with profit. It does mean, however, that every adult must

achieve the feeling of belonging to a *koinōnia*. This may be the congregation in corporate worship, a study group, a church board, a young adult fellowship. Membership may be in several groups at the same time. Through some form of group life each adult will find the satisfaction of his interests and needs for study, work, worship, service, and action.

2. *The Christian movement began as a fellowship, and its "institutionalization" came later.* Through the centuries the church has been most vital when less was seen of the institution and more of the fellowship. We dare to believe that the growing edge of group work with adults is helping us to recover the fundamental role of the church as a fellowship of believers in Christ.

3. *The majority of men and women in our churches have needs that can be met only if they will subject themselves to the disciplines of group fellowship.* So few know how to be a creative member of a group. Everything churches can do to provide group experiences will repay rich dividends of more intelligent and competent churchmanship — more committed discipleship.

4. *Let no Christian boast of his "rugged individualism."* Everything that he believes and practices is a concern of his peers, from whom he receives, to whom he gives; for he and they are bound in the bundle of life, the source and strength of which is Christ the vine and they the branches.

## BEGINNING ADULTHOOD — THE YOUNG ADULTS

" Of all the periods of life, early adulthood is the fullest of teachable moments and the emptiest of efforts to teach." — *Robert K. Havighurst.*

M ost of the denominations will admit that their greatest deficiencies in program are to be found in their efforts to minister to the young adults. This is not surprising when one considers that this may be the most difficult of all periods of life's development to reach with an effective ministry of Christian education.

*Who Are the Young Adults?*

It is even difficult to define who they are. In visiting adult groups across the country, frequently one finds bald heads and not a few gray heads that still go by the name of " young adults." On the other hand the United States Government, in its leaflets and studies in the field of education, classifies all under the age of twenty-one as children.

Earlier in this book it was said that " adulthood begins when life compels growing persons to accept adult responsibilities." This might be called a functional approach to grading, an approach which in many ways is more defensible when speaking of young adults than that of setting arbitrary age limitations.

Traditionally the denominations have graded their materials and planned their programs in terms of age. Those up to eighteen were youth, eighteen to twenty-three were older youth, and twenty-four and above were considered adult. Those who were between twenty-four and thirty, or thirty-five or thirty-eight, or forty, or couples whose combined ages were under seventy-five or eighty, were called young adults. Quite a number of denominations continue to plan programs and write material on this basis, but others have abandoned this age group idea when they deal with adults.

Part of the reason for doing so is that chronological age among adults has less significance than other factors in describing needs, interests, and characteristics. The age eighteen has some validity, for its denotes the approximate time in which most young people in our culture finish their preparatory education. The age twenty-three does not denote a similarly meaningful transition. Nor does twenty-eight, or thirty, or thirty-five. One of the most significant events in the life of young adults is marriage. At whatever age this comes it marks a radical change of interests and living patterns. For this reason some Christian educators are thinking of those between the end of their formal schooling and the establishment of their own homes as a group with identifiable interests and common needs.

If adulthood is marked by the acceptance of adult responsibilities, it is obvious that this happens at an earlier age in some instances than in others. Finding work to provide an independent income is one criterion of arriving at adulthood. To leave home, to assume responsibility for one's own acts and behavior, to serve in the Armed Forces, and certainly to marry and establish one's own home is to enter the world of adult activity and to assume the obligations of grownups. Our culture has accelerated the rate at which the young must accept such obligations. The age at which marriage occurs has been steadily falling, and military service awaits many who reach the age of eighteen. Assuming that those old enough to fight are old enough to vote, it has been seriously proposed that the voting age be lowered to eighteen. College students are thought of as men and women, and servicemen are not addressed as " boys."

It is evident that the young men and women who are in this period of beginning adulthood present a complex picture. Often they are grouped by the simple expedient of marital status. Certainly there is a valid distinction of responsibilities, interests, and needs between those who are married and those who are not. On closer examination, however, the differences are not so simple. Those just learning to live with a marriage partner confront quite a different set of tasks and problems from those with children in school. And among the singles are those seeking a mate, those engaged who for one reason or another are deferring marriage, and those who will not marry at all. From another perspective, young adults can be classified as employed, students, and service personnel. Again these groupings represent valid distinctions in interest and patterns of life, but the picture is complicated by the fact that in each group some are married and some single. Does a married student have more identification of interest and need with a single student or a married employed person of his own age? How do young adults group themselves? These are questions to which we have no clear answers, and much study in these areas is past due.

## What Are Their Interests and Needs?

Despite the complexity of the living patterns of young adults, there are certain common needs and special interests that pertain to all, whether they be married or single, employed, students, or service personnel. This period of transition, from the rather structured pattern of the youth attending high school and living at home to the independent adult who has found his lifework and established his own home, is a time of upheaval comparable only to the age of the junior high youngster who is leaving childhood and becoming an adolescent.

The young adult has to decide upon his lifework, prepare himself for it, and launch his career. He has to select a life partner, marry, and establish a home. He must fulfill his obligations to his country in terms of military service or its options. He must assume a responsible role as an adult in society. He must find congenial social groupings to replace those that are disrupted by leaving home and school. He must assume full responsibility for making his own decisions. For all of this he needs a vital and a growing Christian faith to undergird him. Yet young adults are not found in great numbers as participants in the programs of local churches. This is due in part to the nature of young adults themselves, and in part to the failure of the churches to provide a program that effectively addresses their main interests and concerns.

A group of older youth and young adults, meeting at Lake Geneva in the summer of 1956, pointed out eight areas in which they themselves felt they have particular needs. These were the eight areas: (1) vocation, (2) use of leisure time, (3) setting life goals, (4) achieving emotional growth and security, (5) sex life and mating, (6) family responsibilities and conflicts, (7) facing pressures of a changing culture, and (8) religious and spiritual growth.

These areas of need apply quite generally to the young adult. The student in college may already have decided upon his *vocation*, whereas the employed person may shift from job to job before he finds a work to which he wants to commit his life. Yet the majority of college students change their field at least once and many adults never develop a satisfactory adjustment to the work they do.

With the ever shorter hours of the work week *leisure time* becomes an increasing concern for all of us, but the young person who has severed himself from home and school and not yet assumed the disciplines of a home of his own, has particular perils and needs in this area. And those newly married must begin anew to establish meaningful social relationships.

It is surprising how often young adults raise the ultimate questions in their discussions with one another. They want to know what life is all about: " Why are we here? " " Who am I? " There is deep need to explore the *long-range goals of life* and to establish some kind of working philosophy or to find a framework of faith in which the whole of life can be interpreted meaningfully.

The desire to be independent, to prove his maturity in a set of relationships that are new and strange to him, makes *emotional growth and security* a heightened imperative for the young adult. Although realizing his lack of experience and self-confidence in many areas, he tends to want to hide these deficiencies under a mantle of self-assurance and independence. This paradoxical trait, fairly typical in this period of life, is one of the factors that makes an effective ministry particularly difficult.

Since young adults are of marriageable age it is natural that *sex and the search for a mate* are matters of paramount importance to them. This is not only a thrilling, but often a frustrating and tormenting experience. Though they will admit that they need considerable help in this area, help that is offered is often regarded as unwelcome interference.

The *breaking away from the family* in which one has been reared is often a traumatic experience. Frequently the parents and other relatives refuse to treat the young adult as a grownup. Sometimes when they do so regard him, he behaves like an irresponsible adolescent. The need to achieve self-confidence and independence, and at the same time to maintain his responsible ties with his home and its members, causes much tension and many conflicts. For example, what obligation has a working young person to support a needy family when he wants to establish a home of his own? And when a home is established and little ones arrive, the relationships with grandparents and in-laws are often sources of tension.

The *pressures of a changing culture* bear in upon us all. The young adult feels the urge to make a success of himself and tends to conform to what he thinks society expects of him. The Federal Reserve Bulletin for May, 1955, reveals that two thirds of all the furniture, three fifths of all the automobiles, three fifths of all the television sets, and two thirds of all the washers are sold to persons thirty-five years of age and under. Pressures to adopt prevailing codes of behavior are great, and often in conflict with what has been taught in church and home.

All these areas of need indicate that *a religious faith* which is vital and growing is perhaps the most prevasive need of all. Yet, it is at this point that the church and home seem least effective. Too often the church has tried to reach these people with an extended and slightly modified youth program, failing to recognize that the young adult is quite a different person from his younger brother in high school.

This survey of young adult characteristics and needs makes clear how difficult is the task of enlisting them in active participation in a church program. A further obstacle is their extreme mobility. The student living at home is perhaps the most stable. At least you know his address. The employed young adult not only is prone to change jobs frequently, but when not living at home to change residence as well. Single young adult groups in the larger cities find that one of their major difficulties is to maintain an accurate mailing list, even from month to month and week to week.

Yet these people have recognizable needs and there are ways to plan programs to which they will respond with enthusiasm and devotion. It should be confessed, however, that serious attempts to do so on the part of most Protestant denominations are of recent origin, and none claim a very distinguished record in this effort. The understanding of the young adult and the acquiring of program skill to meet his needs are in process of development in many of the denominations. Through the National Council of Churches considerable experimentation and research are under way. The things that are said from this point on must be regarded as tentative, growing more out of conjecture and projection rather than wide experience and practice.

*Some Guiding Principles for Enlisting Young Adults*

Those who would enlist the young adults in the program of the church must remember that *plans and programs are made with them and not for them.* Not only are they mature enough to have some understanding of their own needs and how to meet them, but to facilitate their further growth they must be given the freedom and the responsibility, to as large a degree as possible, to chart their own course. Young adults do not resent older people taking an interest in their activities, but they do resent anything that savors of the doctrinaire or of the arbitrary use of authority. Being sensitive at this point, they sometimes regard as arbitrary that which is sincerely proffered in the spirit of helpfulness. For these reasons a program, however excellent, that they have not had a part in producing is not apt to be well received.

Another working principle for enlisting young adults is to recognize that *they know they have critical needs and will respect and welcome competent and mature counsel.* It is easy to overestimate the creativity of these persons, particularly in the area of their own religious growth. By their own unaided efforts they can quite capably state their own needs, but to make strides toward meeting those needs requires resources for the most part beyond their experience. If they are to mature religiously, they need the stimulation of new ideas springing from deeper levels of insight and understanding than they possess themselves. This can come from study materials, from new experiences, or from persons of broader training who have thought more deeply; but a group left to its own resources alone is not apt to challenge its own presuppositions. Young adults, therefore, need able assistance in planning a program that is not only relevant to interests and needs, but able to introduce resources to meet the needs and to set the kinds of situations in which change and growth are likely to occur.

Further, to enlist the young adult *a program must be flexible,* taking into account the total scope of his needs. This is particularly necessary because the needs of young adults are so complex, their patterns of living so fluid, and their interests so diverse. For example, the need for social activity is keenly felt by this group as a whole. Frequently the employed have money to spend; they are relatively free from confining responsibilities; they have much of the energy of youth; they are vitally concerned with finding a life partner. The church that would enlist their interest must therefore take these matters into account. This is not to say that program for young adults must be entirely, or even largely, social in nature. It does mean, however, that since the social needs are so important the church that would serve these people must give these needs place in its total program, and show some concern that adequate and wholesome social opportunities exist in the community as well.

The same factors that give rise to a high social interest indicate that young adults possess a high service interest. Often they are impatient with pious talk that fails to issue in observable action. Projects growing out of study and concern will appeal to these people and must be given a significant place in the program. Yet the basic needs for young adults are not met by a full calendar of social events or by a busy schedule of activities. Though they need help to understand, they do realize that they have fundamental anxieties, fears, and frustrations that can only be met when the truth of the Christian gospel is brought to bear upon their lives. This must be accomplished through the most imaginative, creative, and varied approaches that are possible, and even then one cannot hope to reach them all.

*Helping Young Adults to Organize*

Much of what has already been said has implications for the ways in which young adults will organize in the church. Clearly the emphasis should be laid upon program rather than organization. The organization should provide sufficient structure for accomplishing what the group sets out to do. Any more organization than this is superfluous. A committee without a function should never exist.

The steps for organizing a young adult program in a local church can be as simple as the need allows. The following might suggest a way to proceed:

1. Begin with the interested.
2. Confer with the pastor or a representative of the responsible board or committee in your local church.
3. Study your denominational materials and resources for such a group, and try to decide what kind of group you

want and what its purpose ought to be.

4. Make a list of all who might be interested.

5. Plan the first meeting at which your proposals and recommendations can be made to the larger group.

6. Set up the committees necessary to plan future meetings and activities. You will probably need a program committee, a social committee, a service committee, and a publicity committee.

7. When the program is under way, set up a permanent organization with elected officers.

*Relating the Young Adults to the Church*

The majority of young adults are not active in the programs of local churches; neither are their denominational loyalties particularly strong. Therefore, the problem of relating the young adult program to the total program of the local church, the denomination, and through the denomination to the church in its world-wide outreach is an acute one. In Chapter V it was recommended that a young adult should be a member of the adult education committee or council of the local church. This is a matter of the utmost importance and his place on that committee should not be viewed simply as a gimmick to tie the young adult in, but as an opportunity for this important segment of the life of the church to have a voice in determining the policies and programs of the church. There is an impression held by many young adults that when the church shows an interest in them it is mainly to enlist them to do some of the chores that the older members of the congregation would like to avoid. The young adult is not averse to serving, but he would also like a voice in making some of the more important decisions. Certainly those arriving at adulthood cannot bring the breadth of experience and maturity to church councils that their elders can, but often they can and do bring a more daring spirit, a more open mind, and a livelier social passion. Surely without these the total program is impoverished.

We have thought a great deal in this book about the *koinōnia*. Its presence in a church can render an invaluable ministry to young adults. There is nothing the young adults need more than the support of the Christian fellowship. Because theirs is an age of transition, and because they are faced with making so many crucial decisions for which guidance is not easily ascertainable, they often ask questions that their elders regard as impious, and challenge traditions and assumptions that older people take for granted. Rather than be encouraged to " ask," " seek," and " find," too often the young adult is made to feel that somehow he is out of place here and that the church is not sensitive to the things that concern him most. This is also a problem that admits no easy answer. However, if the church is really a *koinōnia,* it will permit restless seekers to make their search within a context of acceptance and love. This, more than any strategy or program, will relate the young adults to the church and advance their maturing in the Christian faith.

## Planning Program

Program for young adult groups must appeal to their interests and address their needs. The general area of these needs has already been indicated. Programs of study, discussion, and activity will have relevance if they deal with matters that are of vital concern to young adults. It is possible, however, to be relevant to needs in program without making very much contribution to Christian growth. This book is written about the *Christian education of adults,* and as Christians we have a responsibility not only to understand and to deal with the needs, but to deal with them in the light of the resources of the Christian faith. For program planners this means that the Bible and the heritage of our Christian tradition will be given a place not only as occasional meeting topics, but as a part of the treatment of whatever subject is being considered, and whatever activity is being planned. This also means that those who plan programs will endeavor always to view what they do with young adults as a part of the total program of the church. The program for any group should never be allowed to become a substitute for active participation in the worship of the congregation and the support of the world outreach of the church through its denominational and interdenominational programs.

## Leadership for Young Adults

Leadership for young adults is therefore a matter of the first magnitude. The most feasible way for the church to provide leadership is through an adviser or advisers. Often a couple can perform this service admirably. Advisers must be persons whose Christian maturity and whose personal competence is such that young adults can sincerely respect them. They must be able to plan and to lead, but they must do neither. Rather, their role is to counsel as the young adults make their own plans and direct their own program. The advisers for young adults must stimulate but not dominate, prod but not prompt, guide but not drive. They must like young adults and have sufficient breadth of interest to understand sympathetically the diversity of their needs.

Where will such leaders be found? Obviously most churches are not overrun with persons of this caliber clamoring for a group to advise. But surely every church has some people with some of the necessary qualifications who can grow in competence with training and experience. The enlistment and education of leaders is adult education too.

Select a leader who is a learner. If he has a love for people, a willingness to study, a desire to grow and help others to grow, and an open mind, he can develop the special skills that the work requires. The committee that asks a leader to accept this kind of responsibility owes him training, resources, and counsel to do the job, and appreciation for his services.

Under the counsel of their advisers and from their own experience the young adults themselves will grow in leadership ability. That they may have the stimulation of other groups, conferences on a city or area basis should occasionally be held under the auspices of the proper judicatory committee of the denomination or council of churches. These are excellent opportunities to share experiences, to exchange ideas, to pool resources and experiences. The main purpose of an area young adult council is not to set up another organization, but to co-ordinate the program in the area and to strengthen the program in the local church.

Sometimes, in small towns or rural areas where most young adults go away to college or to find work, there are not enough in a single congregation to have a rewarding group. In such cases neighboring churches, or all the churches in a community, can sometimes organize an interdenominational group under the auspices of the local council of churches. These provide excellent opportunities for fellowship, service, and growth.

## Young Adults — the Hope of the World

Because adults are slow to change, but the child is plastic and teachable, it has often been said that the young are the hope of the world. The fact is, however, that the primary factor in molding the child is neither the church nor the school, but the home. Therefore, it seems truer to say that the young adults are the hope of the world. They are in transition and therefore quite teachable; but even more important, they have or soon will have the young in their homes.

When the church takes seriously its educational responsibility with adults without relaxing its effort to train the children and the youth, there is real hope that the home will begin to fulfill its responsible role as an agency for Christian nurture. The strategic place to begin is with the young adults.

### RECAPITULATION

1. *Young adults — those beginning adulthood — are in a transition period.* They are leaving youth behind but are accepting adulthood with reservations and often with hesitancy. They know they cannot go back to youth, but the way ahead is not very well charted in a time as unpredictable as the latter half of the twentieth century. These young people need all the sympathy, understanding, and guidance that the church can muster.

2. *The young adult movement has "mushroomed" in many denominations but still needs careful nurturing.* With two or three decades of experience in young adult work, churches now realize better than before how to enlist and utilize young adults in their own spiritual maturing, and how to integrate them into the church. But the going is difficult for churches because so many young adults do not "stay put" long enough to get rooted in local church work. Plans must be made for young adults to have a program that will be sufficiently universal in scope to help them feel at home when they move from Maine to California, or from Texas to Minnesota.

3. *The potentialities of young adults are almost limitless.* When local churches have become aware of these potentialities, their obvious move is to enlist young adults: provide program and resources, with young adults co-operating in the decisions; train leadership; and permit young adults to serve in the church's varied ministries.

Carl A. Rudisill Library
LENOIR RHYNE COLLEGE

## CONTINUING ADULTHOOD — THE MIDDLE AGED

" They who wait for the Lord shall renew their strength,
  they shall mount up with wings like eagles,
they shall run and not be weary,
  they shall walk and not faint."
                                    — *Isa. 40:31.*

*The purpose of this chapter is to explore the interests
and needs of middle-aged men and women, and consider
a program for their Christian education.*

*Physiological Snapshots of the Middle Aged*

" Baldness, bulging, and bifocals " is more than a quip
for men in this era of life. Bulging may respond to diet;
baldness and bifocals are necessary nuisances. Diseases of
the heart and cancer take a heavy toll. Tuberculosis is
manageable. However, with regular medical examinations,
and more efficient surgery, drugs, and remedial care, the
middle aged are in a favorable physiological position.

Women in this period face many of the physical hazards
of the menfolk, and some that are peculiar to the female of
the species, such as menopause in the late forties or early
fifties.

For both men and women, early middle age is a time of
great vitality and physical achievement. Slowly the body
signals the spirit in command to lessen the pace and live
more frugally. Toward the end of middle age, if the body
has been given a fighting chance, it will convey men and
women into promising older adulthood.

*Family Involvements*

If marriage has taken place in young adulthood, when the majority of matings occur in our hemisphere, and if children come, the most of them have been born before husband and wife reach middle age. This is the era in married life when the teen-ager takes command of many homes and gives his parents the most frustrating experience of their lives. In spite of all the truth there is in the slogan " problem parents," there remains a problem teen-ager to be considered and consulted. And the teen-ager is not wholly to blame. He is the battleground of biological and cultural forces that he does not understand or know how to control. His warfare with his parents, teachers, and society in general is but an echo of his battle with himself. (This is not an alibi for all juvenile misconduct, but an effort to be just.)

During middle age the parents strive to make ends meet financially in order to give their children the accepted privileges of our culture. Hazardous temptations assail parents to overwork, to cut corners, to live beyond their income, or to be downright unethical in order to achieve the mythical " success." As soon as one teen-ager is through high school, college beckons, or the Government has needs for his services in the Armed Forces. If there are three or four children in the household, one or more of them is getting married before the parents are out of their forties or fifties. New anxieties arise about in-laws, buying homes, vocational advancement of the married couple, and then — the " threat " of being grandparents. Some welcome this experience with grateful thanks to God; some dread the new status that brings them dangerously near to being " oldsters."

Husband and wife not only have the necessity of rearing and guiding their own offspring; they are under necessity of making adjustments to each other. If the glow of married life is to keep steady, a lot of love must be lavished on each other — not on other men and women. The wife of early marriage has become the mother — not always so handsome and carefree as in courting days, or when fondling her first baby — but surely more attractive *if the husband is a lover.* The husband may have lost his playboy behavior, and some of his physical allurements, but he is the father of her children, the provider for the home, and no one can take his place in her affections *if she is a lover.* Marital counselors would not be working nights to untangle the problems of the middle aged, and divorce courts would have much less to do if churches included more in their programs for the middle aged and their families.

Aging parents present another problem for many of the middle aged. Death, disease, financial disaster, and other causes throw a burden of responsibility on the middle aged who already seem to have enough. But if none of these factors are present, others arise in the field of human equations that can cause problems. Part of the solution rests with the aging, a great deal with the middle aged.

Related to the family involvements are those middle-aged men and women who are single, widowed, divorced, and otherwise. Many issues arise to confront them with spiritual problems that a wholesome church life can resolve. They are part of this family of God that is the church.

### Vocational Situations

Middle age is the period of greatest vocational achievement, or its opposite. A man or woman who has not found his vocational satisfactions in young adulthood may stumble around in a never-ending search to " arrive." Automation and other inevitable changes in business and industry require constant adjustment for millions of men and women. To be unemployed in middle age is a near disaster. Unemployment insurance, social security, and other aids soften the blow but do not completely heal the bruise. Industry and government are not heartless in these situations; neither are they substitutes for a steady job. Fortunate are the middle aged who have found vocational success and can proceed with their life plans.

The church has a stake in the vocational success of its members, and through vocation a man or woman is called of God to serve and witness.

## Citizenship Responsibilities

Society depends on the middle aged for the numerous services in citizenship that community, state, and nation require. Here is the field for the application of Christian principles to the varied needs of all kinds of people and causes. A church that does not encourage, inspire, and dedicate its members to the needs of Christian citizenship, such as office-holding, serving on committees, directing campaigns, law enforcement, and a hundred other responsibilities, is negligent of its duty to its members and to society.

## Leisure Time

People are busier than ever, it seems, but leisure time is available from the shorter work hours, the long weekends, and paid vacations. For a long time churches have been reminded that they are the chief educators of millions of adults to use leisure time intelligently and in the best traditions of Christian stewardship principles. To their dismay, churches are discovering that leisure time creates more liabilities than assets for many of their members. The Lord's Day has become so commercialized in our hemisphere that it is no longer a " day of rest and gladness " for millions of church people, but a " lost weekend " with a serious " hang-over."

We do not want to be guilty of harping on issues that are of little importance, or of overemphasizing the obvious. As people responsible for using time and not abusing it, middle-aged men and women must be challenged to rethink their stewardship of time. With so many worthy causes clamoring for leadership in church, community, and state, leisure time dedicated to a fair share of responsibility is the answer.

Leisure time is re-creational in its potential. People who play work better, think more clearly, live more happily. They owe it to themselves to play purposefully, ardently, joyfully. Play is not a duty to be performed with a wry face, but a privilege that is God given.

The church is a wonderful fellowship in which its members can learn the high values of leisure time devoted to the needs of body, mind, and spirit.

## The Middle Aged and Mental Health

The growth of interest in mental health throughout our hemisphere has scarcely caught up with the pressing needs in this field. Prevention is beginning to receive as much attention as the rehabilitation of the afflicted, who require institutionalizing or expensive psychiatric treatment to resolve the maladjustments. Has the church been at fault in allowing so many of its constituency to lose their grip on life and seek help from others who frequently refer them back to the church for the very help they need? The spate of " peace of mind " books and pamphlets, radio and TV programs on similar subjects, is a phenomenon of contemporary life that demands objective evaluation by the churches. People in such numbers would not throng after mass faith healers, cultists, lift-yourself-by-your-bootstraps advocates, and other questionable leaders, if they were not seeking something to fill the void in their lives. The answer is not invectives hurled at such leaders or the followers who absent themselves from their church folds to listen to the voice of false shepherds. The answer is a better program in our churches to minister to the haunting and real needs of members. Most of those people who stray after these false shepherds have never been grounded in the theological principles of the Christian faith. When churches rediscover the CHURCH, their members will discover the gospel and recover their mental health.

The pastor who has learned the principles and procedures of counseling, and who teams up with the physicians and psychiatrists, and with the agencies of mental health, need have no fear of the false shepherds. The church with a balanced program for middle-aged adults that enlists them will also save them from searching afar, when the resources of peace of soul are so available in their own *koinōnia*.

## A Church Program for the Middle Aged

In sheer numbers the middle aged comprise the bulk of organizational membership. Men's work and women's work, corporate worship, adult study classes, are the fertile fields of activity for these men and women. Church offices and other leadership positions are theirs by right of ability and experience. Obviously, they share these ministries with many who are younger and older than themselves. The mass of middle aged, however, are not in leadership positions; they are the "followers."

The needs of this group have been described in general terms in preceding sections of this chapter. The cross-hatch diagram suggested in Chapter V, or some similar instrument, can be used as a check list to visualize the general and specific needs of the middle aged. From card indexes the information will be available, as well as from leaders who know these men and women at first hand.

The committee on adult work will plan with representatives of the middle aged to outline and develop a program based on identified needs and interests. The ongoing program will be evaluated from time to time. This is essential because of the span of years of the middle aged — from the thirties into the sixties, and because of the changing role of men and women. For example, parents rearing children of teen age will acquire new needs as their children grow, leave home, marry, and establish homes of their own. And if the educational program for the middle aged is clicking, they will be growing and maturing and seeking new outlets for their spiritual satisfactions.

## Grouping the Middle Aged

The standard organizations of most local churches — Bible classes, women's society, men's fellowship, and congregational corporate worship — are the church activities of the middle aged. Participation in these groups varies from church to church, and denomination to denomination. Pastors are happy if they can look into the faces of forty or fifty per cent of the middle aged at times of corporate worship. Bible classes enroll a minority of these men and women in most denominations. Men's fellowships enlist some of the males; the women's society usually activates more of its potential.

As suggested in Chapter VI, " Grouping Adults," there are many needs of men and women that are not being satisfied by our traditional groupings. Either we must readjust the programs of the organizations that are not meeting sufficient needs of their numbers, or we must create new groupings of a more informal nature that will enroll those of similar interests and needs, regardless of sex or age.

The trend in many denominations is in this direction. Liquidation of existing and established organizations is usually unnecessary; enlarging and transforming their programs may be desirable. The answer seems to be informal groupings of sufficient variety to challenge men and women to enlist and keep on learning, and make themselves more competent to witness to their faith. But groups do not come together by spontaneous combustion unless they feel an urgent need to satisfy some lack in their spiritual equipment. This leads us to inquire into the resources that churches can offer for informal groups to study what they most desire.

### What Can They Study?

In preparation for writing this book, denominational adult editors were circularized to ascertain what they had to offer their adult constituencies. All of them mentioned Uniform Lessons as the mainstay of adult study in the Sunday school. Of adults enrolled and using Uniform Lessons, editors reported 100, 95, 85, 75, and in a few cases only 50 per cent.

Those who were not using Uniform Lessons chose electives published by their own denomination, or from other sources. In a few instances, denominations offered adults a comprehensive course of three years, based on careful curriculum planning.

Several editors referred to courses used by adults at other times during the week than the regular Sunday schedule.

These reports do not include courses prepared for use in women's societies, or for church officer training, or leadership education. Sometimes the departments of social education and action issued courses beamed to adults, but intended for use by groups meeting at other times than the Sunday school; or if on Sunday school time, usually the groups were informal and the course was for a short term.

The survey would indicate two things in particular: (1) Uniform Lessons, taught in organized Bible classes, are enlisting the great majority of adults who enroll. However, they enroll a minority of the adult potential in most denominations. (2) Other courses are growing in number, and a sizable proportion of adults are being reached.

The survey did not inquire into the age range of adults enrolled in study groups, but it is a safe guess that the majority are middle aged.

Adult editors were also asked what methods of teaching were recommended to groups. The replies indicated that teaching helps contain suggestions for utilizing the varieties of discussion, role-playing, and other procedures that have been developed in general adult education. The lecture was not condemned, but leaders were being urged to encourage group participation in line with the known laws of learning.

"Group dynamics" was a term still foreign to the majority of leaders of adults in the church school, but many of the writers of teacher and pupil helps were familiar with its philosophy and procedures, and incorporated some of its principles in their writings.

### Do Adults Study?

What has been reported above applies to "study" groups. But do adults "study" even when they belong to a group?

Adult editors were sounded on this question by asking them, "*What home use and class use are expected of adults who are supplied with the lesson periodicals?* "

As to home study, all editors indicated that it was encouraged, but few had tangible evidence to support their hopes. However, many of the pupil periodicals contained clear directives for home study.

As to class use of the pupil periodical, the ruling practice seemed to be that it could be laid aside or left at home without interfering too much with the leader's procedures Does this imply almost universal dependence on the lecture method? If not, does it indicate that leaders of adult groups pay little attention to what the pupil periodical contains, and develop a lesson plan that tries to keep the group interested regardless of educational requirements and objectives? Logic would seem to indicate that a pupil periodical, as well as a Bible, belongs in the Bible-study class.

No check was made with adult editors to learn whether groups using other courses than the Uniform Lessons were utilizing their printed resources at home and in the class. Theoretically, they would make use of these helps because leader and group have come together to study a special subject, and group participation is anticipated. To participate, reading and study are essential. The nonparticipant will lose interest.

One of the bright spots in the report of the denominational adult editors was their feeling (supported by tangible evidence) that adult education was taking hold in their churches. It had been a long time coming but it was leavening the lump of adult potential and slowly lifting the level.

### Leadership Among the Middle Aged

Every denomination is stressing leadership education. The reason is obvious. With the acceptance of *Christian education* as an essential ministry of the church, leaders must understand what *education* is. It is more than a name to identify a study group; the group must use educational principles.

Vast knowledge has been accumulated in past decades about human nature, about learning, and about the importance of the group in the spiritual maturing of men and women. A teacher of a Bible class, an officer in a men's or women's organization, and church officers must be more than functionaries who discharge their duties with aplomb and finesse and piety. The meaning and potentialities of *koinōnia* are too significant to entrust a group to a leader who will not become a member of the group, and who will not prepare himself to use intelligent group procedures.

Leadership education opportunities are available in so many places and at so many times that no excuse is acceptable any longer. Even "natural born" leaders (if such there are) require acquaintanceship and experience with modern educational philosophy and principles to fit themselves for group work with adults.

Every leader must be a learner.

### Outreach of the Middle Aged

The outreach of a local church is an index of its understanding of its mission. If being Christian in all the areas of life is a goal for the individual, it is also a goal for groups of Christians. Group thinking, study, service, and action are forms of outreach to make the impact of the gospel on society and its institutions. The middle aged, because of their involvement in industry, agriculture, professions, and other areas, are "naturals" for extending their witness as Christians. So few of them seem to know how to do it effectively. Through a better use of groups in church life and work progress will be made.

The evangelistic outreach of the middle aged can be greatly increased if they are trained to the task. Although each adult organization has its evangelistic responsibility, some special training is needed for those who serve on the committees. Every Christian is an evangelist by commission of Christ; he needs training and experience to fulfill his ministry. Even Jesus saw the necessity of sending his disciples out two by two to go into all the towns and villages where he was about to come.

How to organize outreach activities will require a pooling of the experiences of the established local church organizations, and the counsel of those who have the know-how in these fields. Calling in a community worker to counsel with adult organizations is one way of training them to be more effective; utilizing denominational leaders in evangelism and social action is another resource. Enlisting those who will take the training is not too difficult if the cause is a responsibility of the church.

*Postscript*

Looking back over this chapter, the mechanics of group work seem to stick out like a sore thumb. Perhaps they have been overemphasized in order to underscore the essentiality of group work. Churches have been zealous to assemble men and women for a multitude of purposes, but have not given enough attention to the psychology of the group, and to its importance for the Holy Spirit to do his work. Everything that has been said in this chapter rests upon the conviction that groups, formal and informal, are the many members of the body of Christ. The nearer they approach the pattern of the New Testament *koinōnia,* the more effective they will be in the program of Christian education — in the teaching ministry of the church.

When a group becomes a fellowship, the mechanics of

group procedure are not noticed by those who are participating. Procedures become ways by which the group thinks and acts under Spirit guidance.

## IMPLICATIONS

1. *The middle aged are the church's backbone in numbers, leadership, experience, and potentialities.* Try sometime to visualize a congregation in corporate worship with all the middle aged absent. Try the same on men's work and women's work, on the church boards, and so on. This is not to proclaim that middle-aged people are more important than other adults; they are men and women without whom the church would be the poorer.

2. *The range of interests and needs of the middle aged is wider than those of young adults and older adults.* The age span, as well as their involvements in so many areas of life, accounts for this range. In this chapter some differentiation was made between those who are recently entered into middle age, and others far on their journey. The local church program will have to give special attention to needs that arise due to physical changes, vocational and leisure-time matters, family affairs, mental health problems, spiritual maturing, and leadership responsibilities.

3. *Study opportunities for adults are increasing.* If a larger number will accept these privileges, and do some *studying*, the hopes of adult education will be realized more quickly. Bible-study groups enlist a large number of adults, and Bible study can come alive if leaders will learn to use group procedures through which the Holy Spirit will guide men and women into all truth.

ARRIVING ADULTHOOD — THE OLDER PEOPLE

"Use us or lose us."
Signed: Your Older People

It takes sixty or seventy years to reach " arriving adulthood," and many older people are seriously inquiring
whether it is worth the effort. What has life to offer when
you are no longer really " needed," but the physicians and
your solicitous offspring insist that you keep on the existence level?

This lament may have had substance up to about the
middle of the twentieth century, but it " ain't " so any
longer. Years before the National Conference on Aging in
1950, sociologists, gerontologists, welfare agencies, and
other discerning observers had been agitating a new look
at the needs and potentialities of older people. The National Conference was a recognition that the time was ripe
for action. Many of the states have legislative committees
on the aging, and other concrete assistance to provide resources for the more abundant living of older people. Local communities are vying with one another to serve the
needs of the aging. " Golden Age " has become a household word to identify groupings of older people for fellowship, encouragement, recreation, and useful service. Numerous funds are available for economic assistance.

Sound psychology and philosophy underlie these programs. They beware of " exploiting " older people; the objective is to enlist them in their own maturing, knowing

well that what is done *with* people is more valuable than what is done *for* them.

Are older people responding? To an encouraging degree they are.

### Church Concern for Older People

It would be unjust and inaccurate to accuse the church of indifference to the needs of older people until spurred into action by Government and social agencies. The church has always had a concern for its older people, and it has welcomed them into membership, visited them when sick, assisted in their financial needs, provided homes for the aged, utilized their abilities, consoled them in their sorrows, bore with their infirmities, counseled them when problems distressed, and helped them sustain their faith until they joined the church invisible.

What has been done will continue to be done. What the church faces now is what society in general is facing in our country — an increasing proportion of older people in the population level. Life expectancy is higher than it ever has been since vital statistics were kept, and the trend is still upward. No statistics about older people will be attempted in this chapter; they would be out of date before the book is in print. Newspapers, magazines, books, and other media can supply live data on the trends in life expectancy. It is safe to predict that everybody is going to live longer than he expected to when he passed the fifty milestone.

This one fact of longer years means that churches will have a larger proportion of older people on their rolls. They will also have a larger potential of older people in their communities who are outside the church. If it was possible to assimilate a ten per cent proportion of older people into local church activities, will it become a burden when the proportion has gone up fifty per cent or one hundred per cent? And what will be the effect on the rest of the program for children, youth, young adults, and middle-aged adults when older people keep coming or, if homebound or institutionalized, still belong to the church's responsibility?

We cannot believe that the church will lessen its concern for older people. But the church must prepare itself to enlarge its ministries. What is more important, the church must help to provide a program for older people that will permit them to carry as much of their own load as they can, and do their best to help the church in its total program. Older people want to "belong," not to be carried on the shoulders of the younger generations as excess baggage.

## Older People Through the Eyes of Younger People

Older people are seldom what younger people see with their eyes. They are both better and worse than seen — better because they possess resources that younger people know little about; worse because older people often try to put up a false front.

When older people live with their relatives, misunderstandings can become unbearable, or understanding can make home a harmony. If younger people would consent to the simple formula, "It is my responsibility to try to understand the older person, and co-operate with him, instead of putting up with him," how different life would become! An oversolicitous daughter whose mother lives with her can make life a continual tension for the mother by refusing to allow her to work about the house at many things that her mother could do and wants to do — not just to help but to satisfy her urge for work and activity.

Young adults and middle-aged adults in their church

programs should have an occasional course on "under-standing older people." The younger would thus prepare themselves for arriving adulthood and, at the same time, learn to accept at full value the older generation. Younger and middle-aged adults combined can " gang up " on older people in the church and outvote and outmaneuver them. They would not think of behaving in so un-Christlike a way if they understood the needs, interests, and potentialities of the older people.

## Younger People Through the Eyes of Older People

Too often older people see younger folks as, " I wish I were twenty-five, or forty, and had my life to live over again." If God had intended life to be lived over, he would have arranged for frequent human reincarnations. God created us to age, and aging is opportunity. Older people should look forward, seldom backward.

Probably the most frequent caricature that older people make of younger adults is to imagine that they are going to the devil. Some older people have not yet discovered that their elders thought the same of them. To trust younger adults is the beginning of wisdom for older people.

Older people may have more confidence in the integrity of middle-aged adults, but too often it is the middle-aged adult who becomes responsible for parents, and unless intelligent efforts are made on both sides, unnecessary unhappiness results. The formula suggested for younger adults might work just as well with middle-aged men and women in relation to older people.

## As Older People See Themselves

Older people are by no means all alike. Age has little to do with the distribution of the God-given varieties of human nature. At seventy we are still possessed of the main characteristics that have distinguished us from all other human beings for seven decades. At ninety, the rule still holds.

If we accept these distinguishing marks of personality, we shall be helped to see ourselves more correctly when we become older people. If we have been quarrelsome, going around with a chip on our shoulders all our lives, we will not suddenly change our attitudes on our sixty-fifth birthday. Conversely, if we have been disciplined by life, we shall willingly and humbly submit to disciplines as we grow older.

In essence older people are likely to see themselves as they have been seeing themselves for many decades. Churches that really " know " older people will take this fact into consideration when developing a program that includes those in arriving adulthood.

### Who, Then, Are Older People?

Churches have had as much trouble in classifying older people as they have had deciding who is a young adult. Retirement from profession or earning a livelihood, if all retired at the same age, would supply a handy criterion for determining that older adulthood had arrived. Fortunately, industry, professions, and the workaday world are not too consistent about demanding retirement at a specified age. (This is said with the full consciousness that age sixty-five has been a kind of standard for retirement.)

In the churches we are not so much concerned with the " age " of older people as we are with ministering to their needs, regardless of whether they are sixty, sixty-five, seventy-five, or ninety-five. Our ministry must be to persons as persons and not to people in brackets or who wear particular age labels. Of course we cannnot avoid observing that aging produces changes in people that make them different from what they once were. Neither should those who are growing older try to deceive themselves and others. Age does take its toll.

Does it make sense, then, to use the term " older people " as *an accumulation of interests and needs that require special consideration in our program-planning?* If this is a true description of older people, then the sting is removed from the epithet "old" that so often carries the suggestion of senility, the scrap heap, uselessness, and childishness. Old people may be senile, or useless, or childish, some of them, even many of them. But society does itself and them great harm by continuing to use the term " older people " to describe weaknesses, when their interests and needs are their really important characteristics.

Such a description of older people takes care of a lot of problems. By concentrating on the interests and needs of older people, churches can form groups in which older people will participate more naturally and profitably. They may desire some groupings for older people only because they do have needs and interests that are common. Another problem this plan resolves is *communication* between older and younger persons in group fellowship. All learn together, the younger and the older exchanging experiences of mutual benefit. The family of God in the church has similarities to the family pattern everywhere, in which grandparents, parents, and children, and all the relatives, have much to contribute to one another.

### Interests and Needs of Older People

Because older people continue to be persons as long as they live, the requirements of their spiritual life are not materially different from those of other members of the Christian fellowship. What the church does for all will be of value to older people. However, it is helpful in program-planning to verbalize a listing of needs to be sure that we know our target — our objective.

Both at the National Conference on Aging held in Washington, D.C., in 1950, and at the International Conference on the Church and Older Persons held at Lake Geneva, Wisconsin, in 1953, a list of basic spiritual needs of older persons was considered. The listing included:

1. Assurance of God's continuing love
2. The certainty that life is protected
3. Relief from heightened emotions (especially guilt, grief, fear)
4. Relief from pangs of loneliness
5. A perspective (for life) that embraces time and eternity
6. Continuing spiritual growth through new experiences
7. Satisfying status in life as a person
8. A feeling of continuing usefulness

Older people who were members of these conferences helped to prepare the listing; hence it has merit as a grassroots statement, and not a patent list prepared by younger people only who " think " these are the needs of older people.

Another approach to understanding the needs of older people is to try the word " adjusting." Older people are compelled to make a number of adjustments, such as:

1. Adjusting to retirement and generally reduced income
2. Adjusting to bodily changes, disabilities, and gerontological diseases
3. Adjusting to loss of mate, old friends, and relatives

4. Adjusting to different housing arrangements
5. Adjusting to one's own age group and to younger age groups
6. Adjusting to the changing requirements of a complex civilization
7. Adjusting to a different role in leadership, vocation, and other responsibilities
8. Adjusting to the inevitable fact of death
9. Adjusting to the acceptance of continuing contribution to citizenship responsibilities in community, national, and international affairs
10. Adjusting to social responsibilities
11. Adjusting to living with oneself

A local church committee on adult work, with similar listings in its purview, will then seek to develop a program that meets these interests and needs of older people.

*Programing for Older People*

In Chapter V, "The Council on Adult Work," it was suggested that a representative of the older people be a member. This was not intended as a "sop" to flatter older people in the congregation, but as an essential representation to build a comprehensive program of adult work. The older person should be experienced, know church life and work, and have the confidence of all the age groups and interests. He has much to give as well as much to learn in the adult committee.

If the adult council has secured a card index of all adults in the congregation, obviously all the older people will be included — those who are able to attend meetings, as well as those who are homebound and institutionalized. These cards will be, in a sense, case descriptions that reveal achievements, potentialities, interests, and needs.

Necessary steps in building a program for older people will include:

1. *What your own denomination is suggesting.* Several of the denominations have issued manuals on older adult work, and more will be forthcoming. These denominational suggestions provide assistance for churches of all sizes and varieties. Plenty of room is left in the suggestions for each church to adapt the recommendations to local situations.

2. *What your local situation demands.* In churches where the proportion of older people to the total membership is comparatively small, no special program may be needed beyond what an alert pastor and an adult council can continue. If the older people are receiving the ministries they need, and are assimilated happily in groups of adults, that church already has a program, and its main concern will be to keep the program fluid to meet new needs.

Other churches may have large numbers of adults in their congregations and in the community. Such a situation may demand several things: ( *a* ) classes and groups especially for older people; ( *b* ) local church clubs of older people; ( *c* ) co-operation with community clubs for older people; ( *d* ) summer camps and conferences for older people, and retreats; and so on.

Such an enlarged program must not violate the privilege and responsibility that older people have to participate in groups and activities of middle-aged persons. A study group interested in learning more about the ecumenical movement, or other world religions, or citizenship responsibilities, or social education and action, seldom should put up a " no admittance " sign to any adult who wants to enlist. Such interests cut across all age lines. Hence there are occasions in which young adults, middle-aged and older persons can profitably meet together for study and action.

3. *Providing leadership.* In all age groupings, or in any kind of adult grouping, leadership is essential. When the adult council has decided that certain groupings of older people are desirable, leadership needs require immediate attention. Suppose that the church sees value in developing a weekday fellowship club for older people: What leadership is needed? Will the leaders be drafted from among the older people, or from younger men and women? What training do they need?

Denominational manuals on older adult work carry plenty of helps to suggest how to secure leaders and train them. The National Council of Churches has also projected a course on older adults and the church, which covers leadership essentials.

4. *Utilizing older people in planning their own program.* Forced feeding may be necessary in some illnesses to keep the patient alive until he recovers his urge to eat. Seldom would "forced feeding" work in a program with older persons (or for any other age group). The more they can be enlisted in planning their own program, the more certain the results. The history of specialized older adult work in churches and communities shows conclusively that older people do not flock like hungry pigeons to any and every "bait" that is tossed to them. First, the church, through its council on adult work, ascertains whether a particular need is unmet. Then the council carries its thinking and factual data to the parent official group. There it is thoroughly canvassed. If approval is given to proceed, the pastor and official boards are consulted to canvass the availability of equipment, expense, and similar items. A planning committee for the special project is created. Older adults are on this planning committee, and

their counsels are heeded. When decisions have been reached, publicity goes out, and the nucleus of a group forms, to grow as interest develops.

5. *Using basic group work principles.* If an aggregation of older people is brought together for whatever purpose — study, recreation, fellowship, service, or any other worthy end — they are a potential *koinōnia.* Basic group work principles apply to all that they do: as they get acquainted with one another, allow the group to set its objectives and plan its program; center the program around persons, with activities as the expression of persons; avoid paternalism; enlist everyone possible in group responsibility; encourage democratic procedures — many in an older group will have to learn how to give and take without destroying the fellowship; move forward but not so fast as to leave many behind; re-evaluate the program from time to time to keep it flexible and growing as new interests and needs develop.

Sponsors and leaders of groups of older people are guilty ofttimes of attempting too much "leading," too much planning, and too little patience. Progress in group work is made *through* people, not by going *around* them. Until the leader has become a member of the group, and a learning member at that, it is questionable whether he *is* a leader.

## Scope of the Program

Churches naturally give priority to the spiritual interests and needs of people. A program for older adults includes everything possible to minister to felt and unfelt needs: corporate worship, prayer, Bible study, fellowship, service outlet, participation, and so on. The ongoing program of a church has already sensed such needs, and attempts to meet them through the established organizations and activities. As already indicated, when unmet needs are discovered, the program will enlarge.

There are other pressing needs of many older people that cannot exactly be classified as " spiritual," but do require competent assistance, such as: financial help; hospitalization when funds are lacking; housing; employment; counseling in particular problems; use of community, state, and national resources; referrals to agencies created to help older people. The local church program for older people will include ways and means of helping to meet these problems. A retired professional man, or a church member who is in welfare work, can be enlisted to give some time to the questions older people are asking but to which they do not know the answers. A church member who is in public-school work, or in college or university circles, can often spark a movement to encourage older people to take courses provided for their continuing education in public schools and other institutions. The growth of the adult education movement testifies to the eagerness and willingness of large numbers of people to enroll. Among these are many older people learning hobbies or achieving skills that can be turned into remunerative income. Many of them simply go to school to learn what they want to learn, regardless of any utilitarian values.

## The Homebound and Institutionalized

Accidents, disease, and other disabilities sentence large numbers of older people to the status of the homebound and the institutionalized. This is not a life sentence to inactivity and uselessness, unless the older person just gives up and withers, or becomes resentful and a real problem " child " for physicians, nurses, relatives, and friends. Experience from hospitals, nursing homes, and other institutions shows conclusively that where the older person has a will to live and improve his physical condition, few disabling diseases, even forms of paralysis, are insurmountable barriers.

A program for the homebound in many churches centers in a "home department" of the church school. Printed materials for Bible study, and inspirational articles in the periodical, carried or mailed to homes, create a group fellowship even of those who cannot go to meetings. Only a few denominations have had the vision to prepare the kind of materials that reach deeply into the lives of the homebound, but more will be forthcoming. Neither have the local churches tapped the resources of service potential that the homebound would be glad to render if given an opportunity. A wheel chair, a crutch, or even a bed of pain can become God's instrument for many kinds of service.

For the institutionalized older people new vistas are opening as denominations and communities restudy what they have, and think ahead for new developments. One trend is to place institutions nearer the centers of activity, where the "inmates" can walk to church and the movies, do shopping, and just window-gazing. Also, more attention is given to leadership for institutions, and programs within the grounds to utilize the potentialities of the members.

The council on adult work has a stake in the institutionalized if members of the congregation belong to this large group of older people.

## Government and Community Agencies

With the growth of the proportionate number of older persons in our population has come an increasing concern among community and governmental agencies. This concern is taking the form of special agencies to survey needs and provide all kinds of resources. Industry is rethinking the retirement principles; gerontologists and geriatricians are working to secure better health services; old-age pensions, social security, and other financial aids are helping greatly; communities go in big for recreational and hobby programs, often centered in excellent buildings; new housing developments, even communities, are enlisting the skills of architects and builders to design what will best accommodate the needs of retired living.

These things are mentioned to encourage local churches to acquaint themselves with the resources, constantly growing in variety and amount, that will supplement the spiritual ministries of the church.

### IMPLICATIONS

1. *An accumulation of special interests and needs is a realistic description of older adulthood.* To try to classify older adults by age terminology is inaccurate because they are not all the same " age " biologically, psychologically, or otherwise. But when certain interests and needs become the common denominator of men and women who are advancing in years, it is right to denominate them as older people.

2. *The resentment of many older people to the word " old " can be resolved if they can be helped to see that aging is God's plan for living.* To be " old " is to keep on fulfilling the last of life for which the first was made. Death is quite as normal as birth in God's economy. And advancing age has a mission all its own when life is dedicated to stewardship living.

3. *A program for older adults in the local church is not something " added on " to keep up with the procession, but the completion of an ongoing program.* Whenever the

needs of older people can be met in miscellaneous adult groupings, this is the approved plan in most denominations. Specialized groupings of older people can be developed when specialized needs are identified.

4. *Older people, whether they admit it or not, require group association.* They can learn to associate with older people like themselves, to become participants in groups below their age, and to engage in community and service agencies. The best insurance against becoming ingrown is to keep growing groupward.

5. *Spiritual maturing is still a goal of older adulthood.* The means of grace are available and, when regularly appropriated, provide the sustenance for growth in grace, and in all the other values of Christian living.

6. *" Use us or lose us " is the challenge that older people are throwing out to churches and society at large.* This is not a threat to secede unwillingly from responsibility, but an urgent request to be employed in the service of God and man.

## QUESTIONS LOCAL CHURCHES ARE ASKING

"Ask, and it will be given you; seek, and you will find;
knock, and it will be opened to you." — *Matt. 7:7.*

For this closing chapter the purpose is to comment on
some of the questions that local churches keep asking
about the different phases of the Christian education of
their growing men and women. The comments will help
to clarify some of the issues that have been discussed
throughout this book.

*Is "Education" an Appropriate Term to Describe What
the Church Is Attempting in Its Teaching Ministry with
Adults?*

This inquiry, as the accompanying letter explained, was
prompted by a desire to find a term that would seem to be
more in harmony with the spiritual work that the church
is commissioned to do. "Education" seems to have connotations that belong rightly to public schools, universities, and the so-called secular schooling, and gives the impression to many that the church is but *imitating* when it
ought to be doing something *unique* and distinct.

The denominational adult editors were circularized
about this question, as they were asked, "*What distinction
do you see between the objectives of church and secular
adult education?*"

Excerpts from their replies reveal to an extent what they

think, and the distinctions that seem important.

a. " Secular adult education is not concerned with the relationship of man with his God, except as indirectly this may be a part of the spirit that is back of the objectives of the secular world. In the church we have the responsibility to help people feel close to God and to express it in daily living. We must, therefore, deal with prayer, so that people may have this connection with the Divine. We must be concerned with the story of the past as it gives to us a pattern for living in the world today, this story being a part of world history that directly deals with man's relationship to and experience with God."

b. " Both aim at learning and growth. Both aim at change — change of ideas, change of habits, change of outlook. Christian adult education has as its specific aim growth and learning in the Christian faith and the Christian life. This is *its* subject matter. But since the gospel is, in a sense, *against* the world, Christian education has in it a sense of transcendent judgment, a dogmatism that is ' out of this world,' which secular education cannot claim to have."

c. " The difference is that the church tries to see all of life in the Christian perspective and uses as its basic authority the Scriptures, whereas secular adult education, although it does not ignore completely this kind of authority, certainly does not make it central."

d. " Secular education aims toward the better citizen in the state. Christian education aims toward the better member of the church, and spiritually, of the Kingdom of God."

e. " I see a great deal of difference. Putting God at the center of life colors everything that the church does. The life and teachings of Jesus are goals as well as methods and, therefore, influence the maturing life every step of the way. The achieving of a Christian life is more than acquiring skills for living daily in our kind of world."

f. " Chiefly the distinction lies in the essentially Christian content of the education sponsored by the church."

Perhaps the replies have helped to clarify the use of the term " education " in church life and work. It is properly called education, but it has unique elements, specially in its emphasis on communication between God and man, its dependence on the life and work of Jesus Christ, and its commission to make disciples who learn to become followers of him who is the way, the truth, and the life.

### Does Church History Belong in the Adult Curriculum?

Many denominations have not attempted to introduce church history into their adult curriculum because they saw no way of making it fit into the Bible-study courses that were most wanted by their constituency. Adults in these courses were content, in the main, to graduate from church history after wading through the Old Testament and The Acts in the New. Their pupil and teacher periodicals made occasional references to church history related to the Reformation and post-Reformation periods, but nothing like a connected presentation.

Some denominations have made church history an integral part of their adult curriculum. They had no difficulty in using the Bible in these courses because the great issues that produced church history were fought out over Biblical doctrines. The result, these denominations believe, fully justifies their efforts. Their constituency learns to appreciate and understand the story of the church through the ages, and the rise and mission of their own denomination in particular. Furthermore, those who are learning church history are better prepared to guide the church in the history it is now making and will continue to make.

One main difficulty to be overcome in introducing

courses in church history is to relate them to the Bible in ways that adults recognize as appropriate and relevant.

*Why Are We Being Urged to Introduce Discussion Techniques in Our Organized Bible Classes When We Are There to Learn the Bible and Not Revise It?*

This inquiry reveals a point of view about the objectives of Bible study. It also seems to assume that the Bible has an authority that man must not " discuss " lest he place himself in a rebel position.

" Learning the Bible " means to many people learning its facts and teachings so as to be doctrinally in harmony with an acceptable orthodoxy. This is good as far as it goes. To others, " learning the Bible " includes the foregoing, but means in addition a response to God's living Word that makes Bible study a contemporary experience with the Divine.

In this latter kind of Bible study, discussion must be used in order to permit each member of the group to arrive at conclusions hammered out in the exchange of experiences, and all under the guidance of the Holy Spirit who broods over such a group to interpret and counsel.

No leader of a group has the right to tell others what to believe about the Bible. He can expound, interpret, explain, encourage, and inspire. All these things he can do better when he combines group discussion with whatever lecturing may be necessary. " Teaching " the Bible can never be dissociated from teaching the people in the group. To ignore their right to learn through participation is a sin to be forgiven.

Discussion techniques do have their limitations. When the issues are insignificant or irrelevant, and when members of the group refuse to adjust themselves to the give-and-take so evident in good discussion, group fellowship dissipates. But these difficulties are opportunities to learn the more excellent way.

Discussion is here to stay. The longer adults resist, the slower will be their progress toward *koinōnia*.

*Why Should a Local Church Council on Adult Work Carry Responsibility for the Entire Church Program for Adults?*

The implication of this inquiry is that a local church committee on adult work might better confine itself to planning for and supervising the adult study classes in the church school.

In some denominations, that is the extent of the responsibility of the adult committee. It is really a committee of the adult department, which includes the organized adult Bible classes only. Obviously, this simplifies its task. It becomes a kind of clearing and steering committee for making more efficient what already exists.

The trend in churches of all denominations is to enlarge the scope of the council on adult work to include in its perspective all the adults of the church — young, middle-aged, older; to be a clearing and steering committee for men's work and women's work, without " interfering " in their unique functions; to consult with the pastor and church officers in the objectives and practices of corporate worship; and to plan for leaders in all phases of adult work, and train them for their tasks.

At the national denominational level interlocking committees plan for all the church's adults. It would seem even more necessary for local churches to unify and correlate their work with adults.

*Who Is Responsible for the Missionary Education of Adults?*

In practice in most denominations women's work accepts responsibility for the missionary education of

women. Men's work in some cases has a missionary emphasis. Adult classes have missionary committees, and many
of them take a share in financial support of particular missionaries. Missionaries on furlough, and staff members of
the mission boards itinerate local churches. All these efforts contribute in one way and another to the missionary
education of adults. To find a way to correlate these activities, and to provide additional opportunities for mission study, is a task that can best be done by having a
committee on the missionary education of adults. It may
be related to the committee on adult work, or to the committee on Christian education, or appointed by one of the
church boards. This committee would promote schools of
missions, family nights on missions, and secure all kinds
of visual aids — maps, movies, filmstrips, displays from
mission lands, and so on. It would also promote study and
reading books on missions, both denominational and others that implement the annual mission themes of co-operating denominations working through the National Council
of Churches. An almost unoccupied field for mission study
is the host of men. When will they be reached?

Several denominations are writing missionary education
into their adult curriculum, both Uniform Lessons and
other courses, and this is probably the most effective
method to reach men and women in study classes.

## How Can Adult Groups Handle Controversial Issues?

Jesus could not avoid controversy; undoubtedly he often
started it. It was one of his ways to get people to rethink
their profession and practice of religion.

If an adult study group should be so unwise as to dis-
courage discussion of controversial issues, it would be going against the very methods that Jesus used so effectively
in his ministry. To try to avoid controversial issues in adult

Christian education is to omit the principal ingredients that produce learning, namely, the elements of weighing evidence and reaching decisions.

Controversial issues arise wherever a group seeks to apply the gospel to specific situations. The main areas of controversy seem to be: race relations; government policies; international affairs; local government; temperance; labor and industry; war and peace; " politics "; and others.

The curriculum that the adult group is studying, whether Uniform Lessons, electives, or otherwise, contains lessons that challenge groups to apply the gospel to their present-day problems. It is up to the group studying this material to learn the methods by which controversy can contribute to learning.

Churches that believe in their gospel commission are convinced that their members, and their leaders, must proclaim the judgment of the sovereign God upon government when it is in error, and upon elected representatives of the people when they are at fault. This will not be done in a personal or partisan spirit, but with prophetic insight and acclaim.

Adult education, whether secular or Christian, has a tremendous stake in citizenship and government. Democracy pretty nearly rises or falls on the activities and intelligence of adults. Men's and women's work and adult groups of all varieties can and should include in their programs many opportunities for their members to study and discuss the issues confronting a democracy. Then they will be better prepared to go to the polls, to participate in " party politics," and to help to make the platforms on which political parties take a stand. They will also acquire the know-how of keeping in touch with their representatives in legislative and executive positions, encouraging them in their fight for good citizenship, warning and advising them when they are on slippery ice.

Some denominations invest money and the skill of competent observers or "lobbyists" to be in the United Nations, and in the state and national capitals, to secure first-hand information and relay it to their headquarters. If the situation demands immediate action by church people, a call goes out to Christians to write, telephone, or telegraph their representatives.

Pronouncements of denominational and interdenominational bodies also serve a purpose by informing government representatives of the thinking and Christian insights of churches. These pronouncements should then become material for discussion in local churches, and especially in adult study groups.

When a denomination has taken a stand on some controversial issue, it is the local church that can make this "stand" mean what it should in the community. If the local church refuses, or side-steps, the opportunity is lost for bringing the gospel to grips with a specific problem.

## How Is Theology Relevant to Adult Christian Education?

Back in the thirties when adult Christian education was becoming a new phenomenon in Protestant church life and work, few of the leaders gave much attention to pointing up the theological implications of the program they were developing. It would be untrue and unjust to accuse them of omitting intentionally this important element, but those were not the days when the churches were recovering and rediscovering theology. The climate has changed. When churches now plan a program for adults, or even for children and youth, they try to make clear the theological foundations on which they are building. They have taken a new look at the church and are sensing that it is much more than an institution among all the other institutions and organizations to which people give allegiance. It is a divine fellowship, a redeeming *koinōnia*, through which God works in Christ and the Holy Spirit to achieve his purpose of reconciliation.

This one fact about the church is not new, but it is new in the sense that we have set our compass to guide us in new directions in every phase of church life and work. We are saying to men's work: "You are the church, the redeeming community, as you carry out your program for men. You are not a fringe group, developing activities that appeal to men; you are the church." The same is being declared to all organizations within the church. And those leaders and members who understand are building on a theological foundation that is Christ Jesus.

Theology about man has been restated. Too long adult work has been limping when it should have been leaping. Men and women have been permitted to assume that if they put forth enough effort, participated in the right church organizations, and maintained decent morals, they were Christians. Christian theology has never taught such doctrines about man, but with the new emphasis in theology, men and women have to face up to what God says they are. They are rebels against God at the best, and traitors at the worst. Only divine grace can make man righteous, and this is a gift, not an achievement. Accompanying these eternal facts are corollaries of significance to adult education: man belongs in the redeeming community and must not thwart his Creator's objective by trying to work out his own salvation. In this divine community — the body of Christ — man has privileges, he has responsibilities. Witnessing is his way of living the Christian life. The group, whether corporate worship, a study class, a young adult fellowship, an older adult association, becomes the church whenever it meets. The presence of a pastor as priest is unnecessary; the presence of the Holy Spirit as Counselor and Advocate is.

It takes whole books to state adquately the theological implications for Christian education. This section has been written to encourage those who read to dig deeper.

## How Is Adult Christian Education Concerned with Creative Arts?

By creative arts is meant the whole range of interests and activities that produce poetry, paintings, sculpture, drama, pageantry, beauty in worship, music, and on and on. The artists who produce these values are meeting needs inherent in human nature. Men and women have response tentacles that take hold to grasp and nurture these precious values.

For Christian education the implications are obvious. People need opportunities to do creative work, and they cannot be satisfied to be spectators only. Every group that enlists adults can make provision for some of its members to attempt the creative expressions that will enrich them and the group. So simple a task as making posters for group needs is a form of creativity. Writing dramatic skits is another. Producing plays, secured from publishers or prepared by a group, develops unrecognized talents. In a leadership course on older adult work in a summer conference one of the members was inspired to write a modern psalm. It was so good that a publisher accepted it. This is an example of adult education.

Not only may adult groups inspire their members to be creative; provision can also be made for learning how to appreciate the rich resources that civilization has acquired. A study of church architecture by an adult group led them to read many books, and to visit other buildings. The became interested in improving their own local church.

Groups that study worship soon discover why divine worship is man's highest attempt to glorify God. As the group takes the historical journey that leads them back and back through the centuries of the development of music, ritual, and other expressions of worship, they go on and on to improve their own worship.

Hobbies are usually creative forms of expression through which an individual or a group does what it wants most to do. Working to make a living ought to bring satisfactions, but hobbies are free from the compulsions of schedule and directives, of organization and administration. Community organizations encourage hobby living, but the churches also have a contribution to make, and the adult program can readily include this creative interest.

*How Are Church and Community Related in Adult Work?*

Every adult who belongs to the church belongs also to the community. Society has accepted responsibility for enlarging its ministries to all its members. Resources covering almost every physical, financial, health, mental, and recreational need of men and women are available from community agencies. Does this leave the church to minister only to the " spiritual " needs of men and women?

Earlier in this chapter a report was incorporated from adult editors who attempted to describe the objectives peculiar to secular adult education, and those distinctive in adult Christian education. It was obvious that no hard and fast line could be drawn. They overlapped. Nevertheless, nearly all agreed that Christian education has to occupy a field for which secular education has no resources.

Omitting for the moment the distinctive objectives of Christian adult education, there still remains much opportunity for church and community to co-operate in adult education. Why should a church develop a program for adults that the public school or higher education can do better? Why should a church feel compelled to give courses in carpentry, home wiring, and a lot of other do-it-yourself skills if community resources make these provisions? Rather, the church can encourage its adults who would profit by these courses to enroll.

Churches often find it necessary to supplement community resources when they are inadequate or nonexistent, but the general rule applies to delegate to the community the major responsibility for mental health needs, employment, financial assistance, play facilities, general education, and other matters by no means foreign to the scope of Christian adult education, but scarcely its major fields.

In these various community agencies Christian men and women will give guidance and leadership, and the churches to which they belong will thus enlarge their service to the community.

## How Are Church and Church School Related?

This question arises because many adult Bible classes (usually men's) are a " church " unto themselves. They offer a program to adults with worship, a " sermon," and lots of good fellowship. Many of the men who go to the class regularly go to the church's corporate worship irregularly.

Perhaps one of the factors that has contributed to this habit among adults is the custom that prevails among children and youth. The church school has become in practice their " church."

This is surely getting the cart before the horse. The church is the body of Christ and the church school is one of the members of the body. Not only should the church be recognized by children, youth, and adults as their spiritual mother; they should likewise recognize the church school and any other organization of the church as a *part of* and not *apart from* the church.

One of the reasons for encouraging the use of the terms " church school" and " Sunday church school" is to give priority in people's thinking to the church. The term " Sunday school," hallowed as it is, means to many people an organization or institution loosely attached to the church. Clearer thinking would compel people to conclude that the " Sunday school" must be the church. Otherwise it will be a substitute for the church when it ought to be the church in operation in one important phase of its teaching ministry.